What's Stopping Me From Being Happy?

Lisa Marie Ellis

◆ FriesenPress

One Printers Way
Altona, MB R0G0B0,
Canada

www.friesenpress.com

Copyright © 2021 by Lisa Marie Ellis
First Edition — 2021

All rights reserved.

Edited by Rosalie Prokopetz

No part of this publication may be reproduced in any form, or by any means, electronic or mechanical, including photocopying, recording, or any information browsing, storage, or retrieval system, without permission in writing from FriesenPress.

ISBN
978-1-03-910532-4 (Hardcover)
978-1-03-910531-7 (Paperback)
978-1-03-910533-1 (eBook)

1. SELF-HELP, PERSONAL GROWTH, HAPPINESS

Distributed to the trade by The Ingram Book Company

*God, grant me the serenity to accept the things I cannot change,
courage to change the things I can, and wisdom to know the difference*

-Reinhold Niebuhr-

Dedication

Dedicated in loving memory of two strong women I had the pleasure of sharing part of my life with. Both women showed me how strong a woman can be when she needs to be. *For my mom (Mema), Edna LeBrasseur, and my mother-in-law, Shirley Ellis.*

Special thank you to my father (Pepa), Sylvio LeBrasseur, for his healing inspiration and endless courage.

With much love,
Lisa ox

Table of Contents

A Note from the Author	ix
Chapter 1: Journey of Self-Discovery	1
Achieving Clarity	1
Exercise 1	3
Discovering Self and Finding Happiness	3
Exercise 2 – Decision Making	4
Exercise 3	12
Living Your Life Your Way	18
Chapter 2: Forgiveness	21
What is Forgiveness?	21
Definition of Forgiveness	22
Holding Onto the Past	23
Letting Go	25
Steps to Forgiveness	31
Exercise 1	32
Be the Master of Your Thoughts	36
Taking Control	36
Exercise 2	37
Chapter 3: Manage Your Stress for a Happier Life	45
Self Forgiveness	50
Chapter 4: Self-Esteem	55
My Self-Esteem Story	55
What's Your Story?	69
The Power of Negative Self-talk	69
Negative Body Image	72
What triggers us to feel more or less beautiful?	76
Positive and Negative Influences:	80
Tips to help you stay balanced:	81
Be Yourself	83

You Control Your Thoughts—They Don't Control You! ... 84
   Staying on a Positive Track ... 85
Change ... 86
   Worthiness Mantra Circle ... 89

Chapter 5: The Importance of Positive Energy ... 91

Negative and Positive Thoughts ... 91
Power of Negative Energy ... 92
Changing Perspectives ... 93
The Power of Positive Energy ... 94

Chapter 6: Self-Care ... 97

   Self-Care Suggestions ... 97
Let's Talk a Little About Control ... 98
Gratitude with Attitude ... 100
More Self-Care Tips ... 101

Chapter 7: The Victim ... 103

Chapter 8: Triggers ... 109

What are Triggers? ... 109
   Examples of Common Episodes that Can Bring Up
      or Set Off Triggers ... 109
   Negative Emotional Responses to Triggers ... 110
   Positive Emotional Responses to Triggers ... 110
Controlling Triggers and Healing ... 112
   Basic Steps to Assist You in Controlling and Helping
      to Heal Your Triggers: ... 112
Boundaries ... 113
Communicate Your Boundaries ... 114
   Boundaries Exercise ... 114
   Boundaries Exercise Worksheet ... 115
   Circles of Life Exercise Worksheet ... 117

I AM Meditation ... 121

About the Author ... 125

A Note from the Author

I would like to thank my husband, Chuck, for all his patience, assistance, and love. Also, thank you to Rosalie Prokopetz for guiding, editing, and helping me complete this beautiful self-help book. I also want to thank my friends and family for their ongoing support. This book has taken me over three years to complete. It certainly took me longer than I ever thought it would. I found myself looking for excuses—or maybe I was just afraid to fail? It goes to show you that even to this day, my learning continues, as does my work on myself. Taking care of yourself, forgiving, and letting go are all parts of a lifelong journey. I am living proof of that. Sometimes you just have to continue to discard your old beliefs and understand what sets off your triggers so you can overcome obstacles with compassion, understanding, and forgiveness.

My goal in writing this book is to help others like myself accept that we are all human, and the work we put into ourselves is all worth it. I want to promote the understanding that the baggage we tend to cling to is just not worth the energy wasted on it. This book is also intended to help raise awareness of the importance of self-confidence and self-worth; to inspire people to do the work and guide them, through the teachings of this book, to understanding and believing in themselves. We can accomplish anything we want. It's all about *choices* and associated consequences.

This book also reminds *me* to continue doing the work. I know the tools provided for you in this book work. I have been using and sharing them for over twenty years and have received so much wonderful feedback from my students. So many strong women and men have changed their lives after letting go of unwanted baggage. The intent is to combine the teachings of the many different workshops I have offered and consolidate them into a single guide for those who want to do the work. It's all in here.

The intent of writing this self-help guide is to reach those that want to help themselves, but struggle to find a clear and consistent method to guide them to a higher understanding of self and individuality. Not every exercise and/or tool will work for everyone, but I hope it will change your perspective or give you a change of opinion to assist you to the next level.

"We can't help everyone, but everyone can help someone." – Ronald Regan.

Be strong, be forgiving, and accept the things you cannot change. Then you will find yourself on a new path, continuing your journey to a new, more rewarding destination.

Remember: you are not alone, and you deserve the very best life has to offer.

Chapter 1

Journey of Self-Discovery

This chapter is dedicated to providing the reader with the following healing gifts:

Clarity. With the gift of clarity, you will notice it's much easier for you to move to the next stage of your journey.

1. On this journey of self-discovery, you will find enlightenment to move you forward, creating a vision and meaningful purpose for your life.

2. We will identify and examine where and how to live your life the way you want to, not the way others want you to.

3. You will also discover what truly makes you happy.

4. You will begin to find the strong unique person within you!

Achieving Clarity

Let's start by exploring what truly makes you happy. Have you ever known or experienced happiness? If you are uncertain or are thinking "not that often," I am glad you picked up this book. Now let's get started and discover what makes you happy.

Most of us live our lives always making sure everyone around us is happy. We assist or enable others to achieve their goals and make their dreams come true. Helping others is very rewarding; however, we need to do it for the right reasons, ensuring we are not over-extending ourselves in the support process. By always doing for others, we tend to forget about ourselves. Women especially tend to put themselves on the back burner. We tend to be caretakers, caregivers, saviours, and mothers to everyone who comes our way. Sometimes, as mothers, we are drained to a point where we are mentally and physically exhausted, leaving nothing for ourselves. Sound familiar?

Many of us have experienced these feelings of being overwhelmed and fatigued. Let's explore some new tools to assist in determining what makes you happy. Most importantly, after doing this exercise, you will also find clarity. This exercise could change your life forever, because clarity is the key word to happiness.

Do you ever feel your life is like running on a treadmill? Are you moving faster and faster, but you're not getting anywhere? It's exhausting to live our lives this way, and many of us do. We wonder why so many have burnout and depression. The treadmill is a horrible way to live your life, and still, many of us continue to live our daily lives in this fashion. If you are beginning to recognize yourself in this description, it means you are identifying the behaviour(s) and are ready to STOP and change your life.

Exercise 1

Let's start with some sample questions. Ask yourself the following:

Am I focused, or do I constantly question the value of what I am doing?

Do I truly know what motivates me and what makes me happy?

Do I have the confidence I need to move forward?

Am I experiencing anxiety or confusion as a result of a change in my life or work?

Do I need clarity with relationships, finances, or work?

Am I feeling off-track and stuck right now?

Am I feeling overwhelmed because I am not clear on where I am going or what I am doing?

Am I trying to find new direction or purpose in my life?

> When you are not clear on your needs, life isn't clear. This brings uncertainty. Negative energy takes over and leaves you doubting yourself, your decisions and your purpose.

Discovering Self and Finding Happiness

The journey to self-discovery takes effort and commitment. You must above all else be honest with yourself: only then can you begin to define those things in life that bring you happiness; those things that give you strength, purpose, and direction. Most importantly, this work will help you gain an understanding of who you truly are and an appreciation for that which makes you unique.

Lisa Marie Ellis

Exercise 2 – Decision Making

What do you see?

How do you feel?

On the next page you will find space to write exactly that.

Take your time and write down the first thought that came to mind when you initially looked at this picture.

_____

_____

_____

How does this picture make you feel?

_____

_____

_____

Are you surprised by your responses? If so, why?

_____

_____

For many of us, our lives unfold in similar fashion to what is seen in this photograph.

We are busy.
We are confused.
We are struggling to find direction.
We are uncertain where to go for assistance.
We are constantly adjusting our speed of life and work-life balance.
We feel we are on a treadmill and always go, go, going . . . but never getting anywhere.

In new situations we struggle to determine WHICH WAY TO GO and can become fearful or anxious.

All too often when we are not ready to do the work, we hop back onto that treadmill because it is familiar and feels like the safest way back to normal. I am sure we can all agree that life can certainly be very confusing and tiring at times.

As you continue to read this book, you will note that I use the word "clarity" often, as this *is* the secret to it all.

Once you are clear on your goals, it is much easier to manifest the life you want.

Let me ask you this: Do you ever feel like a fence-sitter?

Many of us sit comfortably on a fence of indecision, rather than making decisions. Let's explore the reasons why we accept sitting on a fence as a safe position. We will also link this indecisiveness to the cause of unhappiness and lack of clarity.

What happens when you sit on your safe fence? Feelings of insecurity creep in, leading you to question your position or decision. This results in self-doubt, which causes you to start second-guessing everything you do. You become really confused and frustrated, and start to lose confidence. Most importantly, you miss out on so many opportunities. You tend to stay on the fence because you are consumed by the current issue, scared, or unclear of your next steps. In the meantime, opportunities come and go.

Being a fence-sitter is an easy way out. It can provide us comfort and familiar circumstances. We convince ourselves that it's familiar, and we believe it to be a safe position. For those of us who are not sure where we are going, sitting on the fence is a perfect safety net to assist our mind in thinking we are justified or correct. These assumptions can produce the exact opposite result.

Have you ever had a job opportunity and didn't go for it because you questioned your qualifications, education, experience, or another excuse you found at the time? Perhaps the candidate they did select had less experience or was less qualified than you. It happens to many who choose to sit on that fence.

Have you ever gone out and seen the perfect partner for you, but you didn't want to make a move to talk to him or her? Again, by sitting on that fence you could be passing over your partner for life. You will never know, will you? So many opportunities come and go while you are on that treadmill or sitting on that fence. Trust you are reading this book because you are ready for change; you are ready to really get to know yourself and find clarity.

What defines success in your mind? When you see others who you assume are successful, what are you evaluating to support your perspective? They may seem to have the right partner, the perfect job, the beautiful home, financial security, but most importantly, they have found happiness . . . at least from your perspective.

They appear to have it all. The one common factor for successful people is clarity. They are clear on what they want and focus their energy on pursuing their goals without a doubt. They are clear on where they're at in their lives and they manage to manifest those things that may be lacking. In other words, they live their passion.

The word passion has become one of the most popular used words because everyone wants to have that passionate life.

I remember when I first started teaching about passion over twenty years ago; everyone thought I was teaching religion. Today, passion is an overused and confused buzzword. Passion is such a powerful word, because when you truly live your passion(s), you have manifested bliss, a place where we all want to end up before we leave this place.

We all want to love what we do, and we keep hearing, "If you love what you do you never have to work again!" The one way you can get there is to be *clear* on what you love to do. If you're still not clear on what's really important to you today, ask yourself the following questions:

Do I love to be around people, or do I prefer to work on my own?

Do I like the outdoors or prefer indoors?

Do I prefer to have my actions laid out for me with clear objectives and success measures, or do I prefer fewer boundaries and instruction preferring to brainstorm on my own?

Do I prefer to be in a box or outside of the box?

These are just a few examples to assist you in finding clarity.

If you said you don't enjoy being around people, then applying for a position that is public facing and forces you to constantly interact with the public will not lead to long-term reward or happiness. Alternatively, if you prefer to be around others, don't seek a position that pushes you towards isolation like warehouses or factory-line work that isolates you from human interaction for the majority of your day.

Relationships are similar. We often compromise our own needs or our potential partner's needs in pursuit of a meaningful relationship. For example, if you're not a cat lover or you are allergic to cats, you're not going to continue dating a cat owner, as you know he or she loves their pet. It would only be a short-term relationship, as he or she will eventually resent you if they had to get rid of their pet for you. You don't want to change who you truly are or try to change anyone else.

Similarly, if you don't like hiking or you're not an outdoor person, please don't pretend on the first date that you are. Eventually it will come out and once again will result in a short-term relationship. It is so important to be clear about who you are and what you love because if you aren't, I am sorry to say, you will always be living someone else's goals and not your own.

Clarity is the secret to living a healthy, loving, happy life and helps you manifest your long-term goals!

Once you discover your true self, everything comes naturally because you are being true to you! You're not pretending to be someone you're not! Because you know and you are clear on what you truly want, you can now manifest what you want. It's that easy. *Clarity is the key.*

Clarity enhances self-esteem and self-confidence, and vice versa. You need to believe you are truly deserving of your goals and have the clarity and confidence to manifest what will truly make you happy.

Sometimes it's easy to get into a relationship or a job only to find it doesn't last. Ask yourself, "Why is that?" Chances are you weren't sure or clear on what you needed or wanted. I did mention at the beginning you would be hearing the word clarity more often, right?

Have you ever walked into a room where someone's aura, their energy, is so powerful and so attracting that you are pulled to that person like a magnet? That's powerful, isn't it? That person has clarity and self-confidence.

Most of us want to be that person, that someone who has the confidence; the energy of feeling powerful within her or himself. Some might say it's all about ego. Personally, I believe it's not all about doing the right thing at the right time but trusting that you are exactly where you're supposed to be. It's called being happy and fulfilled, after all, isn't that what we all want?

I can't stress it enough that once you have clarity, your goals will all come to you naturally as you will now be living the way you want. Most importantly, you are being true to yourself. So many of us live fulfilling other's wants/needs and pretending to be that someone they want us to be? Are you being the true you? If not, you will always be living someone else's passions. Let me tell you this:

the *truth* always comes out sooner or later! Most importantly, if you become someone else to please the other person, in the long run, you will grow to resent her or him as you will not be happy for long for you are not being your *true* self.

Clarity is the power, and power attracts power!

Do you believe, that you attract who you are and you create what you attract? During one of my workshops, I asked these two questions. One of my students suddenly stood up and shouted, "Are you trying to tell me that I attracted my abusive, so-called husband for the past ten years, the guy who has been beating me and treating me like garbage?" She started crying and ran out of the room.

I had a full class, so I thought I would give her a few moments to collect herself before trying to address the issue. Thankfully, she returned moments later and apologized for storming out. I also apologized and stated we were so sorry to hear that she had been mistreated for so many years. No one deserves to be mistreated or abused. I then asked if it was okay with her to ask a couple of clarifying questions.

I asked, "Ten years ago where was your self-esteem?" I gestured by using my arms at different heights by my side beginning a bit high. "Was it here or this low?"

She acknowledged the level by confirming that it was really low.

My second question was, "Most importantly, back then, did you ever feel that you were worthy of being with someone better than him; someone who would treat you with respect and kindness?"

She started to cry, saying, "It's so true, that she felt that she could never do better than him and that's why she stayed so long in the abusive relationship." The student then realized that it was impossible to feel fulfilled and attract someone who respected her when she didn't respect herself, or felt she didn't deserve any better. It's easy to make empty statements or act in many ways in our attempts to please others. It's important to keep in mind, you truly have to believe you deserve better. As Maya Angelou said to Oprah: "When you know better, you do better."

The room fell so silent you could have heard a pin drop. There were so many in the room that felt the same or were in similar circumstances that they too were coping with. This one courageous participant opening up and sharing her experience caused many others to reflect on what they had attracted into their lives because they too didn't feel worthy or deserving of anything better.

I am happy to say that our courageous participant has since divorced. She is so happy and doing very well. Since the workshop, she has returned to school and is feeling confident about her decisions. She is clear on her goals and her direction.

This is why it is said, "You attract who you are." That is, you attract the circumstances in which you find yourself. So, as of today, start paying attention to what you are attracting into your life. This is, again, so important: be aware of your surroundings, your environment, your friendships, your job, etc.

If you want a better friend, then be one. If you want the partner that will treat you with respect, then start treating yourself and them with respect. I think you get the picture. Once again, if you are clear on what you want and need, you will attract it.

I think by now you are clear on the importance of being clear. Now you want to know how to get clear in all aspects of your life, right?

Exercise 3

To get the list going, let me ask you the following questions:

First ask yourself, what's missing in my life?
What do I need to improve?
Am I being true to myself and others?

Next, ask yourself, what's important to me at this time in my life? Is it:

My work?
My relationship with family or friends?
My present relationship with my partner?
My finances?
My health?
My hobbies?
My spiritual life?
My environment?
Something else?

For whatever outcome you desire for whatever you have identified as important to you, start with what is most important to you right now. Before you start, however, you need to truly *believe* you deserve it. *Feel* it.

Clarity is the secret to living a healthy, loving, and happy life! No matter what it is, if it's important to you, then please take a moment to write it down. You are worthy.

The mind is a powerful thing, and we can convince ourselves that what we truly want isn't that important. We may justify why we are not deserving of it.

Ask yourself, what is it I love to do? What is the one thing I think about that instantly brings a big smile to my face?

Please take your time and write five important things you want to see and/or have happen in your life. Nothing is too big or too small. Don't limit yourself. Trust.

Important things I want to see and/or have happen in my life:

1.
   _____

   _____

   _____

2.
   _____

   _____

   _____

3.
   _____

   _____

   _____

4.
   _____

   _____

   _____

5. _____

_____

_____

You now have clarity on what makes you happy and you have just written your top five goals, which will help you on your journey to happiness and contentment.

Let me provide another real-life example from one of my workshops. One of my clients kept pointing out she wanted to find a partner who would treat her well and respect her. She further explained that she really wanted a relationship. The odd thing was once we started the workshop; her need for a relationship wasn't even on her list of goals. I pointed this out to her and said, "You keep saying it's important to you to be in a good relationship, yet it's not on your list." She had no explanation and was clearly surprised.

What I am trying to emphasize is that even when you think something is important to you, when you really take the time to think about it, things that may have seemed top of mind, might not be as important as you may have originally believed.

I also asked this individual, "What are you doing to find this right relationship?"

She replied, "You're right. I never went out looking or put myself out there at all. I really didn't try to start a relationship, so how could that ever have happened?"

We all tend to make ambiguous statements of wanting one thing or another. However, when it comes right down to it, it's really about being definitive, making the effort, and gaining clarity to focus on what is truly important. Recognizing that needs do change, it is important to assess against your list of goals. Decide if your needs have really changed, or if you are trying to fill a void in your current life situation. Remember that old saying, "Be careful what you ask for, as you might just get it." –Unknown Author

Ask yourself this: "What do I think has been stopping me from achieving my goals?" You have taken the time to discover your top five goals, and you are telling me these goals are important to you! So, what are you afraid of?

Please go through each goal and answer one at the time. (E.g., my first goal is finding the right partner. What's been stopping me? I don't leave my apartment to meet anyone, as I don't have the confidence. I haven't told anyone I'm single again, as I am afraid of getting hurt again, etc.)

What I think has been stopping me from achieving my goals:

1. _____
_____
_____

2. _____
_____
_____

3. _____
_____
_____

4.

5.

What do I need to do to fulfill my needs and wants? (Do I need to return to school to get that better job I want? Do I need to feel more confident and believe I can do this? Do I need to volunteer to get the experience?) Whatever steps you need to take to accomplish your goals, write them down.

What I need to do to fulfill my needs and wants:

1.

2.

3. _____

_____

_____

4. _____

_____

_____

5. _____

_____

_____

You can establish a list of goals and write them down so they become a reference and form a commitment to you. You have now written down what is truly important to you. You trust yourself that you will do your best to make this happen. Remember, this list defines what's important to you. Important to remember, you deserve it. Now, go make it happen! Congratulations! You have clarity in your life.

Living Your Life Your Way

The next step toward finding happiness is changing your way of thinking. You must believe you can make this happen. These goals define what is important to you. You need to create new thinking patterns in your life. If you've been going without what makes you happy, find the sources of distraction.

Is it a lack of confidence?

Do you not believe you deserve it?

Are you not worthy?

Is it a lack of funds?

Whatever it is, you know you can lessen the source of distraction and make it happen.

Trust, believe, and have faith. Remember, you deserve it!

Depending on your generation, we have all experienced negative influences and beliefs. The Baby-boomers were raised with many negative thoughts. Do you remember hearing some of them?

Money doesn't grow on trees, you know.

Don't jinx yourself.

You have to work hard to make good money.

These types of influences impede our pursuit of dreams and goals.

If you do something right, recognize it and acknowledge your achievement, celebrate it and reward yourself. Own it! Be proud of yourself!

If you love what you do, you never have to work again.

Yes, they are right about money, it doesn't grow on trees, but if you're doing what you love to do, money will come. It will. Trust it.

Now that you have completed the work in this chapter, you now know what has prevented you from realizing goals. You now know how to move forward. I like to think it's like a map—you now have your map to do what makes you happy! No more excuses. You have what you need. Now get off that treadmill, and no more fence-sitting. You are ready to finally focus on your goals and make yourself happy.

As we know, it starts from within. Money, material, and someone else won't make you happy. You must make yourself happy; then the rest follows and continues to support your happiness.

Just remember: you attract who you are. Look around and start paying attention to what kind of friends you have around you. Who are you attracting these days? Do these individuals support or enhance your ability to achieve your goals and support your overall wellbeing?

You now have clarity on what makes you happy.

No one is stopping you but you. Sometimes we all experience periods in time where circumstance force us to lessen our focus on our goals. Remain committed and stay on track to keep progressing! Believe you will and you will. Trust yourself and have faith.

Now let's move on to the next chapter and work on releasing what is no longer needed. This is the gift of forgiveness.

With much love
Lisa ox

Chapter 2

Forgiveness

Forgiveness is not something you do for other people. We do it for ourself to get well and move on.

What is Forgiveness?

When you think of the word forgiveness, what comes to mind? Take a few minutes to contemplate this and write down your thoughts.

_____

_____

_____

Definition of Forgiveness

"Psychologists generally define forgiveness as a conscious, deliberate decision to release feelings of resentment or vengeance toward a person or group who has harmed you, regardless of whether they actually deserve your forgiveness.

Just as important as defining what forgiveness *is* though, is understanding what forgiveness is *not*. Experts who study or teach forgiveness make clear that when you forgive, you do not gloss over or deny the seriousness of an offense against you. Forgiveness does not mean forgetting, nor does it mean condoning or excusing offenses. Though forgiveness can help repair a damaged relationship, it doesn't obligate you to reconcile with the person who harmed you, or release them from legal accountability.

Instead, forgiveness brings the forgiver peace of mind and frees him or her from corrosive anger. While there is some debate over whether true forgiveness requires positive feelings toward the offender, experts agree that it at least involves letting go of deeply held negative feelings. In that way, it empowers you to recognize the pain you suffered without letting that pain define you, enabling you to heal and move on with your life."[1]

---

1   The Greater Good Science Center at the University of California, Berkeley, (2020), Forgiveness Defined, What is Forgiveness. Retrieved from https://greatergood.berkeley.edu/topic/forgiveness/definition#what-is-forgiveness

Holding Onto the Past

How do we feel when we don't forgive and refuse to let go of our old baggage?

Frustrated Angry Traumatized Out of Control

Anxious Attacked

Stressed Addicted to that Situation

Unworthy Low self-esteem Depressed Ashamed

Suitcases labeled: Guilt, Depression, Shame, Triggers, Forgiveness, Self-Esteem (Past / Love)

Are any of these feelings familiar to you?

So many of us waste so much time and good energy talking about our past experiences, reliving it, and reflecting on it. Let's not forget how much of our feelings and mixed emotions we choose to hang onto from our past. Why? What a waste of good energy, don't you think?

Hanging onto old unresolved baggage stops you from moving forward and stops you from being the best you can be. Forgiveness . . . a gift to you.

Many of my clients say "I don't want to forgive that person for what she or he has done, because if I forgive her or him, I feel it gives them the right to continue to treat me poorly and excuse them for what they have done."

It's definitely never okay to hurt anyone. However, holding onto that negative energy and all that hurt gives that person control and power. You are allowing them to continue to have power over you.

By not forgiving, you are still allowing that person to control you and continue to hurt you in so many ways. Don't you think it's time to take back your control and stop wasting your time and energy on her or him? Haven't you wasted enough time and energy by now? How long has it been since you've been hurt? How many times have you stayed awake at night thinking about it and feeling angry or hurt? How many? How many times have you sat at your dinner table or in bed and wasted good times reliving that episode again and again, carrying all that weight from your past?

This is all in the past. There is nothing you can do about it to change it. What you can do to help yourself is to change how you react to that incident. You can't change people, no matter what they have done, but you can change how you react to it all.

I recall a client who kept coming to me as she felt so stressed. Most of her stress was caused by the way she reacted to her husband's stress. She wasn't aware of it, but she in fact chose to take on his stress. As she explained it, her husband continued to come home from work and complain about his day at work, especially about his boss who he detested. Each night he would eat dinner with the family and go on and on about his boss and how she treated him. Of course, she and the children always walked on eggshells as they never knew what kind of mood her husband would be in when he walked in the door at the end of each day.

So, one day I asked her, "If your husband detests his boss so much, why does he keep bringing her to dinner? Why does he keep bringing her home and continue wasting his energy and ruining your dinners, etc.?"

Letting Go

When you think about it, how many times have you wasted your energy on someone that you had an issue with or someone who has hurt you in anyway? Think about all the times you thought about that person who has brought hurt and damage to your life and self. How many times did you bring that person to dinner or to bed or to your family functions? How many times did you take it out on your loved ones when thinking of that someone? Or a trigger that went off and you don't know why? Each time that unresolved emotional trigger goes off you are once again giving them control as you have not resolved and healed that time in your life. That time in the past.

Are they truly worth all that time and energy? Of course not! No one is worth wasting your good energy on a negative experience!

Haven't they done enough to you yet? It's time to just let it go and release the pain once and for all. The best way to do this is by forgiving him or her. I hate to say it, but I bet they don't think of you or waste their time talking or feeling concerned about you. Because you forgive doesn't mean you forget, but again it will be your choice to reminisce on that time. Remember, it's your choice to let it go. No one can take that away from you.

The beauty of forgiveness is that once you forgive, you heal yourself. Once you heal yourself by letting go of that negative energy, you then heal everyone around you. You will notice, that the energy of anger, frustration and ugliness goes away. You feel the peace of releasing, of forgiving.

Look at every occurrence in your life as an experience. See what it has done over time and you will come to realize that every experience has made you the strong person you are today. It has made you the special individual you have become. Let go . . Let God... let your

Higher Power take over. Release and feel the difference when you finally stop inviting that person into your life. Remember, each time you allow those triggers of negative emotions to come into your life, you are once again allowing this person to take over your feelings and use your energy. They're not worth it. Let go of their negative energy. Let go, and leave it to your Higher Power.

Everything you hold onto affects your life (negative or positive), including any past dysfunctional relationships, verbal abuse, physical abuse, or psychological abuse, etc. If you let it, every negative experience takes a hold of a piece of your mental and physical energy and your life.

Emotions and feelings influence thoughts and give them energy. What kind of energy do you want to hang on to? What you put your energy to will show up!

Thoughts and feelings go back and forth. How many sleepless nights have you wasted on thoughts and feelings about someone or something you have no control over? What I mean by no control is you can't control what has already happened to you. You can only control how you keep reacting to it. Does this sound familiar?

"To forgive is to set a prisoner free and discover that the prisoner was you"

– Lewis B Smedes

Let's try to figure out why we choose to not let go. Not letting go or not forgiving must serve some purpose.

What is your purpose in life? What are you gaining from it?

_____

_____

_____

Why are you sticking to your old story? After all, you can change your story and create a new one? You are the author of your life! Why do you choose to keep that old hurtful story?

_____

_____

_____

Why are you not letting go of the pain? Why do you choose to keep all those triggers active? Why do you want those feelings to keep creeping up in your life, time after time?

_____

_____

_____

Are you getting attention from others by keeping this story? After all you certainly have been giving it a lot of attention for a long time!

_____

_____

_____

Do you like the drama? Many people only live in drama. It seems they're not happy unless they have drama in their lives.

_____

_____

_____

Do you like being a victim? If yes, why do you choose to stay a victim? Once again many do, as they don't know who they would be otherwise. This has kept them where they are in life.

_____

_____

_____

Is this your excuse for not moving forward? Why do you choose to keep this excuse?

_____

_____

_____

What's it doing for you? Ask yourself that question.

_____

_____

_____

Why do you want to hold onto your anger, hurt and everything else that is keeping you stuck in the past? Holding on to unhealthy memories and feelings are only hurting you, not them. It's an act of violence toward you! Once the action is over, it no longer exists unless you choose to keep it alive. Why do you choose to keep this trigger, this pain alive? Why? To forgive is a choice! It's *your* choice!

By choosing to hold onto this pain you will continue to attract those kinds of people.

You attract others based on who you feel you are!

Negative memories that keep on running and running through our heads . . .

Feeling Angry

Sleepless nights

Migraines

Feeling sad

Why me?

Arguments

Many days ruined

Frustrated

Stuck in my past

Forgiveness helps us clear these out.
The work is worth it!
You control your thoughts. They don't control you.

Steps to Forgiveness

"Know exactly how you feel about what happened and be able to articulate what about the situation is not okay. Then, tell a couple of trusted people about your experience.

Make a commitment to yourself to feel better. Forgiveness is for you and no one else.

Forgiveness does not necessarily mean reconciling with the person who upset you or condoning the action. In forgiveness, you seek the peace and understanding that comes from blaming people less after they offend you and taking those offenses less personally.

Get the right perspective on what is happening. Recognize that your primary distress is coming from the hurt feelings, thoughts, and physical upset you are suffering now, not from what offended you or hurt you two minutes—or ten years—ago.

At the moment you feel upset, practice stress management to soothe your body's fight or flight response. Give up expecting things from your life or from other people that they do not choose to give you. Remind yourself that you can hope for health, love, friendship, and prosperity, and work hard to get them. However, these are unenforceable rules: you will suffer when you demand that these things occur, since you do not have the power to make them happen.

Put your energy into looking for another way to get your positive goals met, rather than through the experience that has hurt you. Remember that a life well lived is your best revenge. Instead of focusing on your wounded feelings, and thereby giving power over you to the person who caused you pain, learn to look for the love, beauty, and kindness around you. Put more energy into appreciating what you have, rather than attending to what you do not have.

Amend the way you look at your past, so you remind yourself of your heroic choice to forgive."[2]

Exercise 1

Who has disappointed or hurt you in anyway (even if they are no longer living)?

_____

_____

_____

What have they done to you that you need to forgive them for?

_____

_____

_____

1. How do you *feel* about them?

_____

_____

_____

2. What do you *think* of them?

_____

_____

_____

3. How do you feel they have affected your life or health?

_____

_____

_____

4. What must happen with them in order for you to let it go and be happy?

_____

_____

_____

5. What triggers do you think you have been storing because of this experience?

_____

_____

_____

6. What is it you want from the person who hurt you?

_____

_____

_____

7. What have you learned from this experience?

_____

_____

_____

8. What advice could you offer to your best friend if this was their story?

_____

_____

_____

9. Now, I want you to go over your answers and really think and feel. Write down what has come up for you (no judging).

_____

_____

_____

You may notice that your answers are most likely negative. This is negative energy that you have wasted time on and are still wasting time on today. Do you agree? I now ask you:

Do you think this person thinks of you as much as you do of them?

Do you think they are worth all the energy you expend on them?

Do you think spending all this time thinking of them and having those negative thoughts and feelings gives you or them power?

By spending all this time thinking of them and having those negative feelings and thoughts do you feel that you are hanging onto their crap, their baggage?

Do you think what they have done to you has been done to them?

Is this enough for you to let go, knowing that maybe the same has been done to them at some point?

Can you find some kind of empathy for that person?

Do you believe it's time to release those negative thoughts and feelings once and for all?

If you answered yes to any of the above, take your paper with all your answers and burn it or cut it up into tiny pieces as you let go, forgive, and release the pain and negative thoughts to mother earth, knowing and trusting she will heal it all.

Be the Master of Your Thoughts

You control your thoughts. They don't control you.

Once you control your thoughts, your feelings will be in control. You can then master anything you want. You can choose to be happy, compassionate, loving, contented, whatever you decide.

Once you decide what you want and why you want it, it is easier for you to move on. Your path becomes clearer, and you can become the best you can be. Once you choose to let go of that piece of the past you tend to be more in the "now," no longer wasting time and energy in that old story from your past.

Once you trust your higher power and trust that you are exactly where you should be, everything else just shows up the way it should. Trust, have faith, and let go.

Many people say they have faith in whomever or whatever they have faith in and yet they continue to doubt that they are exactly where they should be. This leaves me questioning whether they really do believe. Faith is believing and accepting that you are exactly where you should be. Not trusting keeps you living as a victim. Trust that everything has happened for a reason and it's made you the strong individual that you are today. Keep in mind you are exactly where you should be and let go.

Be in the now: that's known as being in the state of being.

Remember, your thoughts shape your life.

Taking Control

What do you want to be? What kind of life do you choose to have from this day forward? Say goodbye to your old story and welcome the new one.

Be in the now. Open your heart and connect all your best parts together. Be open and in love with your tomorrow. Let go of yesterday's story. Start fresh. What does being happy mean to you? Sometimes we keep ourselves so busy that we forget that what we are teaching or preaching isn't what we are living.

Exercise 2

Ask yourself the following:

Who do you want to be?

_____

_____

_____

Who did I used to be?

_____

_____

_____

Who am I today?

_____

_____

_____

Who do I want to become?

_____

_____

_____

What do I need to change to become that person?

_____

_____

_____

When I wake up in the morning, what do I want to *see*?

_____

_____

_____

When I wake up in the morning, how do I want to *feel*?

_____

_____

_____

When I wake up in the morning, what do I need to do?

_____

_____

_____

Ask yourself, how do I want to start *thinking*?

_____

_____

_____

How do I want to start *feeling*?

_____

_____

_____

Be mindful, how do I want to start acting and behaving?

_____

_____

_____

Be in touch with your soul, unlocking and unblocking the true you, not fitting into who you think you should be or are expected to be. Let go of your ego.

Heal your past. The present will unfold in a much happier way. Stop carrying that heavy baggage which no longer serves you.

Feelings and emotions are the biggest energy users. Our energy is connected to all our past experiences negative or positive. It does take work to release and face it all, but that's how you heal. Otherwise, you will be carrying that heavy baggage forever.

It's your choice. Once you connect to who you want to be, you then break the familiar feelings, and let go of those damn triggers that come up unexpectedly. Most times, facing the truth does hurt as you might discover you're not who you thought you were. Once you get there, take ownership of everything, and I mean *everything*, from your past. Confront your feelings and respond to your triggers. Then and only then will you connect with your soul. Remember, your emotions and experiences are a part of your soul.

If you are ready to truly be connected to your soul in a healthy way, then let it all go and be the true person you want to be, not what others think or want you to be. If you don't heal it now, those crazy triggers that bring up anger, jealousy, depression, and ugliness will continue to be a part of your heavy baggage. These triggers will follow you from one relationship to the next. I can almost guarantee that you will continue to attract those who hurt you or make you feel inadequate or whatever you are feeling about yourself. Remember: you attract who you feel you are.

If you don't heal those triggers from the past, they will continue to come back and affect your life in a negative way. Who knows, you might even want to keep yourself busy so you don't have to face who you've become. That's the reason many are addicted to technology, excessive shopping, drugs, alcohol, prescription drugs, sex, thrills or anything to numb the feeling or state they are in. All these addictions you might *think* make you feel good at the time, but we all know it's all a temporary fix.

Ask yourself: what rush are you seeking to ignore the deep healing? How do you keep yourself busy?

It's not your fault; most of us don't even know we are on this path of self-destruction. We just do it because it feels good. It fills the gap and helps us to feel numb. These temporary fixes are a means to ignore what is really going on in our life. We also ignore what we are really lacking in our life and within us by substituting the healing for a temporary fix or blaming others for where we have ended up.

Now that you know, and you are taking this precious time for *you*, it is time to address all these triggers, past issues, and old baggage we tend to hang onto. Should I go on? I think you get it. Addiction is often caused by failing to deal with or heal from a past emotion or experience. Many of us deal with fears, low self-esteem, anxiety, depression, guilt, and anger daily.

It's time to ask yourself which triggers are affecting you on a daily basis. What feelings come up that stops you from moving forward? What triggers do you need to deal with to be able to face today? Ask yourself what feelings come up that affect your relationship(s) including the relationship with yourself? How do you treat yourself?

Is today the day you finally let go and face it all? Why not today? Why keep prolonging it if you know it will continue to show up again and again? If you choose to ignore it, maybe the next trigger affecting you will be that much stronger.

When you look at your life, think of how much time and energy you wasted on her or him, or your family, a friend or a co-worker? How much time and effort have you wasted? How many times have you tried to change someone who has hurt you or want to punish them in a certain way?

Think about it. How can you be living your life to the fullest when you are stuck in the past? You can't be in the moment. You can't be living the best you can be if you are not in the here and now because you chose to stay in your old story. Do you get it?

Why waste all your good energy on something that you can't change? Why continue to give those who hurt you the power to influence your feelings, your life? It's time to finally let it go and live the best you can. It's your choice.

Once you release your past story, just think of how much more energy you will have to give to your present and future. How much more joy you will have, and how much lighter you will feel. Feel the freedom of letting go and forgiving. Give yourself a present: be in the present.

Family members, friends, and coworkers can set off our triggers. We then become desperate, guilty, ashamed, helpless, victimized, etc. You get the picture. Let go of your past. When you think about it, what are you getting from holding onto it? Is it control? Are you still trying to control that time, that emotion, that negative familiar feeling? By letting go of the control, you let go of that emotion clinging to you, unless you choose to hang on to it. It's *your* choice!

By focusing on the future, you can now be more motivated and inspired with new goals. What normally comes next is gratefulness for where you are going. Automatically, you are in a new story.

You control your thoughts! They don't control you.

Do you want to master your life? The only way you can master anything is by doing it over and over and over again. Remember to give yourself a break. You have been living your life for how many years in this way, clinging to the past? You need to take baby steps.

As of today, and each morning going forward, you will choose to wake up and see yourself and life in a totally different way. You will begin each morning stating at least five things or feelings you are grateful for.

What's Stopping Me From Being Happy?

I am so grateful for _____

I am so grateful for _____

I am so grateful for _____

I am so grateful for _____

I am so grateful for _____

As of tonight and each night going forward, before going to sleep you will choose to go to sleep with gratitude, either by writing or stating five things or feelings arising out of your day for which you are grateful.

I am so grateful for my day because _____

I am so grateful for my day because _____

I am so grateful for my day because _____

I am so grateful for my day because _____

I am so grateful for my day because _____

Gratitude with attitude will create your wonderful new story. Be open to watching your new story grow and blossom.

With much love
Lisa ox

Chapter 3

Manage Your Stress for a Happier Life

In this chapter, you will discover techniques to manage your stress and increase your wellness. As we all know, once you learn how to release stress, you then have time to focus on the now and be a much happier you. Many call it "bliss;" a place where we all want to be.

In my experience, when my clients come to me regarding anxiety and guilt, most of them are thinking of and living in the *past*. When they come to me talking about how stressed they are, they are mostly thinking of and living in the future. Does this make sense to you? From now on, when you feel anxiety or stress, stop and think about where your thoughts are. I wouldn't be surprised if they are in the past or future.

As I mentioned in Chapter two, "if you truly believe and have faith in your higher power" I mean truly believe; wouldn't you trust that you are exactly where you are supposed to be in life? You are supposed to be right *now*, in the present. When you think about it, all your choices have brought you *here*. This is the consequence of the choices you make!

Remember in the first chapter I stated that one thing you do have is *choice*. No one can take that away from you. Every choice has a consequence. Every choice also gives you an opportunity to decide how you react to what has happened. Whether you decide to stay in this situation or continue and move on, it remains your choice.

If you trust and have faith, then you must truly believe that you are exactly where you are supposed to be! Yes?

If you are at a place in your life that doesn't feel right, then ask yourself the following questions:

What choices did I make in my past to get me here?

___

Why am I here?

___

How did I get here?

___

Do I feel like anyone has contributed to my present state?

_____

_____

_____

What have I learned from all my experiences, if anything? Some people choose not to learn and just remain a victim. Again, that is your choice. You must accept the consequences of your choices.

I have learned . . .

_____

_____

_____

Trust and just stop trying to control where you need to be or better yet, where you want to be. Trust and just let go. Stand back and take the time to make the right choices. Really learn from your past patterns, and let go of your old beliefs.

Let your higher power assist you. Trust, and really think about the answers you gave above. Sometimes we need to write things down to see the truth, to understand and learn from it.

Were you able to answer any of the questions? If yes, good job! Don't forget to give yourself a pat on the back for all your hard work!

Keep living in the present and try to catch yourself when you are dwelling in the past or stressed about the future; work to come back to the present. Reassure yourself that for whatever reason, you were meant to take that path, to learn what you needed to learn. Also remember: that's your old story.

You are reading this book for a reason. You are ready to better yourself and gain clarity, releasing what is no longer serving you. It's time to be the best author of your new story, your new journey, by making the right choices. By actually living in the now you will really let go of so much stress. After all, the past is the past. You can't change a damn thing. But you can change how you react to it today and from this day forward.

I'm not saying this will be an easy task. Whenever you feel you don't want to be where you ended up, even for a moment, ask yourself, "How did I get here? Where are my thoughts? What choices do I have?" Even for a second, if you are in the wrong place, take the time to ask these questions of yourself. Discover the negative triggers that brought you there. It's always so much easier to attract familiar situations, especially if you didn't heal those old emotions or triggers.

Think back to what has been going on. What have you been attracting?

_____

_____

_____

Does history keep repeating itself?

_____

_____

_____

You are not the only one who does this. It's so much easier to follow old, negative patterns rather than digging deep and doing the work required to create a new you. Let me tell you, it's all worth the work that is unless you want to continue with your old patterns and keep the lifestyle you are in. After all, it's *your* choice.

We sometimes keep piling up the hurt and disappointments storing them deep inside us. It's a lot of work to dig down deep and damn; it hurts to open up deep wounds! Also, blaming others for where we have ended up is always much easier than looking at ourselves and taking ownership. Don't you agree?

Today you have made the choice to read this book. Today you have made the choice to change your patterns. Today you are choosing what's best for you. Either way, it's your *choice* with all the consequences attached. It all depends on which direction you are choosing to follow, negative or positive. We all know the choice I'm rooting for!

Allocating blame happens when you find yourself saying things like "It's your fault I didn't succeed," "It's your fault I quit school," "It's your fault I got sick," "It's your fault I didn't do this or that." Be careful when you point your finger of blame at someone else, as there are three fingers pointing right back at you! Try it now! Point at something or someone and see for yourself. Is it time to take ownership of who you've become; of where you are in your life? If you agree that you are ready to take ownership, then keep reading.

Taking the time to heal what has been buried is the one way to finally stop attracting the same damn thing or person into your life. Those things or people that you don't want bring you stress repeatedly. Change your patterns, change your life! Are you ready to take ownership and move forward to discover who you really are? You are a strong individual. It's time you started seeing yourself that way. Let's continue and do it together.

Keep in mind, releasing stress can also be as easy as going for a walk, doing yoga, meditating, exercising, journaling, playing, or listening to music, and so much more. You choose what can help you release stress.

Now, let's continue to dig deep down and heal! I am so proud of you. You have chosen to continue to do the work. It's time to forgive yourself. After all, it starts with you. Healing and letting go will assist you on your journey of healing.

Self Forgiveness

1. How have I disappointed or hurt myself?

_____

_____

_____

2. What actions or decisions have I made that I need to forgive myself for?

_____

_____

_____

3. How do I truly feel about myself?

_____

_____

_____

4. Who am I when no one else is around, and do I like that person?

_____

_____

_____

5. What actions do I take when others are around, and is there a difference? If yes, why?

_____

_____

_____

6. Why do I feel so guilty?

_____

_____

_____

7. What is it about myself that needs to happen in order for me to let it go and be happy?

_____

_____

_____

8. What triggers do I think have been stored because of my experience?

_____

_____

_____

9. What advice would I offer my best friend if this was his or her story?

_____

_____

_____

10. Go over your answers. Take your time and write down the feelings that have come up, feelings you have been hiding (no judging).

_____

_____

_____

It's time to review the advice you would give to your best friend. Maybe it's time for you to become your own best friend and take your own advice.

Do you believe it's time to release those negative thoughts and feelings once and for all and stop beating yourself up over and over again? You can't change your past; you can only change the *now*. Accept the person you truly are. Love yourself unconditionally.

> *I am that I am.*
>
> *– Exodus 3:14*

Just remember this competing can quickly turn any relationship into an ugly battle. Can you possibly be a winner, if it is at the expense of making others losers? Solid relationships are built on sacrifice and caring, not power and control. Competitiveness can drain the joy, confidence, and productivity from any relationship

Take the sheet with your answers and *burn* it or cut into tiny pieces. Release the pain and negative thoughts to mother earth knowing and trusting she will heal it all.

Good job! Now give yourself a pat on the back for doing this hard work. You are so worth it.

With much love
Lisa ox

Chapter 4

Self-Esteem

Self-esteem can be an ongoing issue that we must work on. Let's be honest, we can be our own worst enemy! Right?

High self-esteem or low self-esteem is not gender specific; it affects men and women alike.

My Self-Esteem Story

I would like to start by sharing my personal story, which is the reason I love to teach and address the issue of self-esteem in this chapter.

My story of low self-esteem started as young girl, at the age of seven. I was born in Quebec in a little village called St. Jogues. It was a peaceful, beautiful, little and "out of this world" type of place. At least, I always thought so. In this little town we had one little store called Oneille's General Store. It had anything you could possibly think of, especially lots of candy. I remember the entrance had a wooden screen door with a spring. As a little kid, if I didn't run in quickly enough, it would hit me from behind. This store also included a single gas pump for fuelling cars, tractors, and snowmobiles.

Across the street from the store was the most beautiful church you have ever seen—or at least it was to me. Today, when I go to visit that church, I can still spend hours and hours in its calm, peaceful energy. I'm sad to say that in 2018 they started locking up the church for the first time, due to it having been vandalised. Prior to this, the church had always been open and available whenever needed. My Aunt Geraldine LeBrasseur has been managing and volunteering at the church for the past twenty-five years. Let me tell you she ensured the church was spotless. She recently retired in 2019. Everyone was sad to see her go. We were all grateful for her long-time love and commitment.

The whole community knew one another. Every Sunday, my family would meet at my grandmother's house for a homemade luncheon after church. All my cousins, my aunts, and my uncles would be there. I now wonder how my poor grandmother ever managed to feed us all faithfully each Sunday. I must also say these meals always included fresh baked goodies, delicious pies and lots of great homemade bread. I will always cherish the many beautiful, warm, loving memories made there. We were all so very close.

It was a town where everyone trusted one another and always helped each other whenever needed. I don't ever remember there being attention paid to money or materials back then. I just remember we had what we had. We just didn't know any better. We were happy with just being together. We never went anywhere outside of St. Jogues and that's all we knew.

We didn't have much money, but we were rich in so many ways. We never noticed the poor part. I don't remember ever going without, not ever. We had our own farm with lots of animals to feed us. My mom made most of our clothing, and my dad hunted and made sure we always had food on the table. We picked a lot of blueberries and wild strawberries with our mom whatever was in season at the time. We were out there picking and then making jams or whatever else my mom and older sister, Sylvie could create. My family consisted of my mother, Edna, my father, Sylvio, my older sister, Sylvie, and two brothers, Langis and Gaétan. We were a very close family, and to this day I am happy to say we still are.

I was seven years old when my life changed drastically. We had a house fire. I saw my home burn down to nothing, as if it had never even existed. I will never forget that day. It was devastating to see everything just burn away. We lost everything. I was so amazed even at that age that our lives could change in one day. Our beautiful home, everything my mom and dad worked so hard for, had all just vanished, just like that. That's how fast one's life can change.

When the fire was going, I was told to run and go across the street to our neighbours and stay there. So, I did. I ran upstairs to my girlfriend's bedroom with Guilainne and Anna. From her bedroom window we watched as everything burned down. I remember we were crying and wondering where we were going to live. My friends asked, "What are you going to do?" I felt so lost and scared. We all did.

To make a long story short, somehow, we ended up in Niagara Falls, Ontario. My dad knew there was work there in construction. Of course, in those days, they never asked a child if they minded. You just followed. We never really knew what was going on until it was time. Children had no voice and were not asked for their opinions back then. Children were seen but not heard. The only thing I was happy about was this was going to be my first train ride. Imagine a little girl that had never left her little village, ever, and now was travelling on a train to this big city called Niagara Falls. Wow, that was certainly something new in our lives. I never knew anything about this city, nothing except that there were all sorts of people and they spoke English, a language we knew nothing of.

Putting the excitement of the train ride aside, I never ever wanted to leave our little village and our family. I wanted to be with my family and of course had no choice.

It was so sad saying goodbye to all of our family and friends. The whole town was sad to see us go. I remember getting on the train and hearing "à bord" (all aboard)! I then saw so many different people from different racial backgrounds, something I had never been exposed to before. It was intimidating in so many ways, yet exciting because of the unknown and the anticipation of what I was going to see and experience next. From the time I left, I already missed my memé (grandma).

Our train ride took twenty-four hours. We finally stopped and exited the train on Bridge Street in Niagara Falls. I remember the conductor saying "Niagara Falls," as I didn't understand anything else he said in English. I do remember thinking to myself, *So this is the big city*? I guess everything was really big for me at that time, especially the fact that I had never really seen big buildings and so many stores, hotels, cars, and even a big blue bus. We had a black and white TV but never watched it, as we were always outdoors, so we hadn't seen much of anything growing up. Our experiences were limited to our little village and what we learned in school. This entire change was devastating. I didn't understand what was truly going on. As a child, I had no choice but to just carry on and do as I was told.

Losing our home and the only place we knew of was very scary in so many ways. Within this whole mess, another tragedy happened really quickly; my parents split up too! Wow, I thought I knew moving here was going to change life as we knew it, but didn't realize it was going to change our family as well. In those days a marital break-up wasn't the thing to do. You were disgraced. Trust me we had enough to worry about as kids, but again it just happened so fast. I guess as a kid I never saw the signs. I was young. I felt so lost but it seemed like my older siblings were okay with all this change. Maybe I was so consumed with my own hurt, that I didn't ever consider their feelings, or perhaps they didn't show it. I am sure they were being brave to protect me. I was the youngest one and just wanted to be held and be told, "It's going to be okay." This never happened, and it was never okay after that.

At such a young age I knew what I was feeling just wasn't okay. I just didn't know it was called fear and low self-esteem. I had never seen the world so sad and cruel. I was so scared in this big city knowing that nothing was ever going to be the same again. All I ever wanted was to go back to my little world, my little St. Joques where I felt so safe. I just wanted us to be the family we used to be.

We ended up moving into this little apartment, a sad little apartment on Queen Street for those who know Niagara Falls. There were many little dives above the stores downtown and we lived above a Metropolitan store in a two-bedroom apartment, which meant we had to share one room, separated by a sheet. I think that's what it was; the boys on one side and the girls on the other. I remember climbing so many stairs and walking down a very long hallway to get to the end of this old building to reach our little apartment. There was no going back. Let me tell you, for all of us that had to be the most challenging part. When we lived in St. Joques, we were always in the woods if we weren't at school. I'm not ashamed to say that I was a bit of a tomboy and enjoyed playing in the woods. The only yard we had now was the rooftop of an old store. I remember on hot days in the summer you could smell the tar and sometimes it would stick to our shoes, but that was now our new yard. When I look back it was so dangerous to play up there, as it had no railings. It was an open roof with just building after building. Keeping in mind I came from a place where we were never inside, we were always out in the forest. This was just not fun for any of us.

The best part about down East was that my parents never had to worry about us, as everyone knew each other. Some days we would go off for the entire day. My sister (Vivi) Sylvie would pack a picnic. We would go into the forest and build a house. We even used to make a small fire and have hot tea. My sister was very responsible. She was the best!

As for Niagara Falls, that was not the case at all. There were so many strangers and the traffic was brutal; for us any traffic would be. I actually had to look both ways before crossing the road. Back home all I had to do was to listen for a car coming down the gravel roads from the distance, which was not too often.

Niagara Falls was such a big city for me. Everywhere I looked, every word I heard, and any sign I saw was all in English. Of course, everyone we met spoke English. It was so difficult of course as we didn't understand a word of English. At least my mom put me into a French school, called St. Antoine for which I was so happy as I got to speak French.

There was so much bullying there for me. When I first started there wasn't a day that I wasn't called shorty, French fry, frog, or poor kid, and with my parents now separated, it was brutal. Again, more beatings on my self-esteem, and I was declining more and more.

I remember some days coming home from school and feeling so sad. One day as we were walking down our long hallway a door opened. There were many apartments along the way to ours. There stood this elderly little woman as short as me. She came out to greet us and asked in French how our day went. I was so stunned that she spoke French. Then she offered us a peanut butter and banana sandwich. She was so sweet, and this made me feel as if I were back home. I think at the time she just reminded me of my grandmother who I missed terribly. I was thrilled that I had found another little old grandma. To this day, I adore the elderly.

After that day, she would come out and greet us often and always offer her famous peanut butter sandwiches. I could tell she was also lonely, but my youngest brother Gaétan and I loved the attention.

Even at my age I knew she felt so sorry for us. She was so good to us all. She lived with her only daughter and her little bird. She knew we were lost in this big city, and she knew we didn't know anyone around us.

As time went by it got rougher not having my dad around. I missed him, my old friends, and mostly my grandfather and grandmother. I really missed country living.

I recall one time when my mom sent my brother and I across the street to buy a deck of cards. We had to cross Queen Street to get to the store called Gold Variety Store. Of course we searched and searched in this big store and couldn't find the cards anywhere. This meant, I had to now try to communicate with the cashier to find what I needed. I tried to explain it with my hands while speaking in French. Finally, I grabbed a pen from the counter top and drew a spade and heart! She finally said, "Now I know." There was a long line up of people waiting in the store and making fun of it all. They and the cashier were laughing. I was so devastated and ashamed because I didn't know how to speak English. I am sure the cashier knew what I wanted but wanted a laugh on me. I often wondered why this was happening. Why? We were so happy in St. Jogues, or so I thought. Why did this have to happen?

I did not feel too good about myself. Years went on and I really missed my dad, as I didn't see him as often as I would have liked. He was busy with work and his own life too. I grew into a teenager, and as we all know when dads are missing from a daughter's life, we tend to look for that man's attention, somewhere and anywhere else. For me, I married the first man who said he loved me. I was only sixteen years old when I married. I really just wanted to be like my brothers and sister and be married. Imagine getting married at such a young age. Even back then, in 1978, that was not a normal occurrence. As a matter of fact, my mom had to come with me to the City Hall to sign my marriage certificate, as I wasn't sixteen yet and we needed the certificate ahead of time for the priest to marry us. I turned sixteen in July and was married in August 1978.

I have to say, that the best thing about my getting married, was that my mom and dad got back together after the wedding. After all those years, they reconciled. I always knew they would for some reason. I always knew deep down they were meant to be together. That was the best gift God could have ever given me at the time. I would do it all over again just for that.

I was trying to be very mature for my age. My husband at the time was nineteen years old. I felt marriage was the only thing I knew and was taught. School wasn't talked about much, and it didn't seem to be an important issue in our home. I remember down east it was believed that a woman's role was to have kids and care for them and the man's role was to work to support their family. If a woman was in her late twenties and not married back then, they started calling her an "old maid." So, I honestly felt that my duty as a woman was to get married and have children. That's all I wanted. To my surprise it didn't work out that way. God had other plans for me.

When we married, we were so young, and of course it wasn't a healthy marriage. How could it be at our age? There was a lot of verbal abuse, and some physical abuse as well. Money was always an issue. My husband was a workaholic, and material possessions were very important to him. He was always trying to "keep up with the Joneses." This was how we lived. We first moved into a little apartment and one year later we bought a house with a big mortgage and a lot of responsibilities.

The house had to be spotless and dinner on the table when he got home. I dropped out of school, of course, because I was now married and had more important things to do, or so I thought. I started working full-time at a factory, which didn't last long. Actually, any job I had, never lasted. Big surprise, I was never happy with any job! I just didn't realize that I couldn't be happy with anything when I wasn't happy with myself.

My job was not my main focus, even though I found one job after another, as we needed the money. I was married now, and all I wanted was to have and care for children. Of course, that was now my new job, my duties as a woman. The problem with that is it didn't happen as I planned or believed it would. We tried and tried to get pregnant. We tried tracking fertility using the thermometer and anything else the doctor suggested.

Once again, I was devastated and not feeling like a real woman; all I thought was that I wasn't even good enough to have kids. What was wrong with me? What kind of a woman was I? My self-esteem was so low: I didn't need my husband putting me down too. I was doing a great job all on my own. We were two kids trying to live in a grown-up world. After two years of being mentally abused and abusing myself, I finally got pregnant.

I was the happiest woman around. I was finally doing what I was put on this earth to do—be a mom. I started decorating my baby's room, which I had been planning almost my whole life. It was all bright yellow, so perfect. Too perfect. I was eighteen at the time, and then the saddest thing happened: at four and a half months I had a miscarriage. I thought my life was over. I went into a small depression and again started beating myself up with negative thoughts. I never felt as lonely in my whole life as that day when I lost my baby girl. I even went through labour and delivered a stillborn little girl.

I experienced so much sadness as I felt I had let myself down as well as everyone else. I remember for months afterwards my stomach was still so big that the mailman asked me how far along I was now, he had no idea I had miscarried. My self-esteem was as low as it could possibly get at the time, or so I thought. I didn't even want to go out anymore until I lost my weight and boy did I lose that fast. All I ate was bananas and toast for months. I felt so ugly and less of a woman. I was really struggling with self-esteem issues. I felt my body wasn't even good enough to carry a baby. I felt my body had really let me down. I kept asking myself what was wrong with me. It was hard on both my husband and I as that's all we wanted, children. Well I certainly did, that's all I wanted without a doubt. I think I needed to do it to prove that I was a woman, because if you get married, the next step is having kids, nothing else. That was how I had been raised. I couldn't stand it when I would encounter people I knew and hadn't seen for a long time and they would ask, "So when are you starting your family? I am surprised you don't have any kids yet."

Another two years passed and I was seeing doctors, taking my temperature and doing the whole bit again to try to get pregnant. More and more, I felt less of a woman. Marriage was difficult, more fighting, more stress, and more yelling. Somehow in all this mess, I finally got pregnant. I was unable to do anything while I was pregnant—doctor's orders. However, she was worth it. We had a baby girl and named her Trisha Marie, the most beautiful girl in the world. I was so happy to have my little girl. She was the world to both of us. The doctor told me not to have any more children as I almost died delivering her. I was thinking that couldn't be right. I had to give my husband a boy, as that's all he wanted now, a baby boy. Did you know they used to call it the "million-dollar family"? Of course, or so I thought, that once I have a boy that would be the perfect picture, the perfect family.

My husband wanted a boy so badly. I thought I can do this, even against Doctor's orders, I can do this. Once again subjecting myself to more mental abuse for a number of years. Three years later I became pregnant again. I miscarried again. In the meantime, I suffered so much mental abuse, never feeling good enough, never having enough love in the family. Let me tell you it wasn't just about having a baby by then. This just wasn't right. Then it happened: I got pregnant again. I'm not sure how I carried this little one, as there was so much fighting and arguing within our marriage. I was stressed to the max. I almost lost him a few times and was so surprised I didn't miscarry. He was a miracle child. The stress that we needed to have a boy was an added pressure. When I look back, I am saddened to say that it was unhealthy to live this way, live on demand. At that time, I was never sure that my husband really wanted any more children or if he just wanted a boy, so he could say he got what he wanted a boy. I remember he was also always being teased by people saying, "You better get that boy!" Maybe it was just me finding another way to see myself as a failure and to beat myself up. Who knows?

When my little boy, Jason Sylvio, was born, our marriage wasn't the same at all. Things got even worse. Although I thought it couldn't get any worse, it did. I remember the lady in the room next to mine at the hospital had her husband there visiting all the time. I was so envious of their relationship. As for me, it was just my little one and

I. Back in those days they kept you almost a week in the maternity ward. I really missed my daughter and just wanted to go home to be with her too.

As time went on over the years, the marriage got worse and worse. I had done what I thought I was put on this earth to do. A woman gets married and has children. Don't get me wrong, I love my children! They were my life, all I had.

As more time passed, I found I wanted more for myself. It just wasn't enough being a wife and a mother anymore. I love my children, however, I knew there was something missing and for once I thought I needed more for *me*. That's when I realized, I was finally thinking of my own happiness. Imagine that.

You know what they say: "When the student is ready, the teacher will appear," and so it happened. I found myself getting a part-time job as an assistant at a beauty salon. The owner was the most wonderful woman I had ever met. Her name was Carmelina. She was a strong woman in my eyes. She had her own business, and let me tell you her husband George, was not her boss, he was her partner. I saw that loud and clear. I came to see a new way of living, and I loved it.

Carmelina's customers were all women, and they just loved me. They gave me so many compliments each day and this made me realize that I am okay, and not that bad. I also made good tips and now had money of my own. I only worked three and a half days per week and the shop was just down the street from where we lived. Trisha was in school for half a day and Jay was in daycare half a day while I worked. I wasn't *allowed* to hold a job if my husband had to "babysit." Thinking back, fathers should never refer to watching their kids as "babysitting." I had to make sure my little job never interfered with anyone else's plans or I would be forced to quit. That was also loud and clear. I loved going there, I was learning so much from those strong women. I was so naïve. I didn't really know anything about being a woman. Didn't I just become one once I married and had babies? I was a *woman*! Wow, that's what I thought.

Let me tell you, even after having two children and being married ten years I think it was this job that helped me became a woman and helped me to understand how strong a woman can be. I realized a woman can do what she wants and doesn't need a husband to do it for her. Let me tell you, this way of thinking didn't just happen overnight. However, I found myself taking strong baby steps forward.

I wanted to go back to school, but didn't, as it would be too much for the family. I was reading self-help books purchased at garage sales and starting to help myself. All I wanted was to be recognized as one of those strong women, like the women at the salon. Of course my husband didn't like it when I started working there. I started speaking up more, doing more, and being more adventurous and courageous. I found myself a new girlfriend, someone to talk to, and she lived right next door. I was growing stronger and stronger as a woman and becoming a better example for my children.

One day I woke up and thought, *this can't be all there is to life, it just can't be. I can't continue to stay in this relationship, or whatever it was at the end.* Somehow we had managed to stay together ten years, more than I ever thought the marriage would last. We stayed together for the children, what a big mistake. I knew I was broken and needed time to repair. Once again, I was feeling that I had failed at my marriage. I knew deep down I had to separate to find myself and become stronger.

We finally separated after being married for ten years. The children and I moved into our own place. Keep in mind; I had never lived on my own so it was pretty daring of me to go through with this. At times it was very scary for me too. I never let it show even through many hard times. When I look back, I had my two-year-old son on my hip and my daughter who was six. When I told my parents I was leaving my husband, they couldn't believe it. They didn't want me to because we had a nice home. I don't think they believed I could do it on my own with the children. Somehow, material possessions were also very important to those around me, myself included. I just didn't realize it at the time. Looking back, the home that I shared with my husband was perfect on the surface. The state of my home was the only thing I had control of. I was keeping the house clean and making sure the kids were great and never went without. You couldn't have found a cleaner home anywhere, and the kids were my life. I was told so often that this was my duty as a woman, I almost continued to believe it . . . almost.

Finally, we divorced, and our family home was sold. Of course, it wasn't a pretty divorce. I was the first one to be divorced in my family, this was yet another big disappointment to them. I felt everyone was looking down on me with shame and feeling so sorry for me, now a single mom with two children. I knew this was for the best as it wasn't a good atmosphere for the children; the yelling and the constant fighting was horrible.

The children and I moved into a subsidized rental unit. It had three bedrooms and it certainly wasn't like our big house. It was actually more like one-third of the size, but we made it our beautiful, happy home. I *loved* it! For the first time in my life, I had my own space and could come and go as I pleased. I was in charge and no one could tell me what to do, when to do it, or how to do it. I found myself wanting to return to school. Anytime I had a chance, I would read many self-help books. I felt my self-esteem rising a bit but understood that I still had a lot of fixing to do. I was still so down on myself.

Years went by. Of course I was young, and I got into another relationship. What kind of man do you think I attracted next? . . . The same kind, which is no surprise! Right? If you don't think you deserve better, you will *never* have better! Again I was in a relationship for two years with a very controlling jealous man. I guess I still hadn't learned. One day my life finally changed. I found myself attending a retreat on "forgiveness" hosted in Mount Carmel, Niagara Falls. Well, that changed my life. I finally forgave my children's father and most importantly, I forgave *myself*. From that day forward my life changed because I changed. I truly believe that when you heal yourself, everyone around you heals! I didn't want another man in my life. I finally got it—I didn't need a man in my life to be happy. I just wanted to be on my own with my children. I finally realized I could do it by myself with my children. I got a good job at a call centre and was then able to purchase my first home. The children grew up. It wasn't easy being a single mom, trust me; it was difficult being the full-time mom and dad. Their father never bothered with them and let me tell you, I paid for that many times over and over again. However, by forgiving myself I can say, "I did the best I knew how." Do I have any regrets? Of course I do! Could I have been a better mom? Of course I could have, but I'm just easier on myself now. I always remind myself that I did the best I knew how and was able to do as a single mom. Time went on, and I found myself drawn to helping at women's shelters and volunteered there whenever I had time. I tried my best to help those women stay out of abusive relationships.

Years later, I went back to school because I found myself wanting to teach. Attending that retreat on forgiveness is what helped me with my story. I always used to say that I would return to Mount Carmel to teach, and I am happy to say that I have done so, many times. Each time I still cry, as I cannot believe how I have changed since the day I walked into that centre. It had taught me how to forgive and be kind to myself. Twenty years later, I am thrilled to say that I now teach various topics about helping yourself and healing your inner child.

I changed, accepting who I was. I finally took ownership of my life and the person I have become. I started trusting who I am and that I am where I am supposed to be. I needed to let go of control, of who/what I felt I should be or how I was told I should be! That was a hard one. Some days I still work on that, but that's okay too.

The best day for me was the day I came to realize that I didn't need a man. I also knew by forgiving, I would be opening up space for love, peace and happiness, Years later, I found the right man or he found me. His name is Chuck, and at the time he had a seven-year-old son, named Royce. I truly believe they came when I was ready, when I knew I deserved better and knew I didn't need a man (husband) to be happy! I finally got it, you get the better of everything when you *truly believe you deserve better* and not until then! If you don't believe you deserve better, you will continue to attract whom and what you *feel* you deserve.

We've been together now for over twenty years and married for over fifteen years. I truly believe I deserve what I now have. When you become a better person, you attract better people. I am also happy to say, I also have five beautiful grandkids, Jade, Cossette, Makena, Jude, and Reece, who we love dearly.

So, that's my story. That's my truth.

What's Your Story?

We all have one, after all.

Now, let's get ready for you to start the work!

The Power of Negative Self-talk

Let me ask you these questions:

How important to you is your image? Why?

On a daily basis, how much energy are you wasting on perfecting your image? Who are you trying to be or look like?

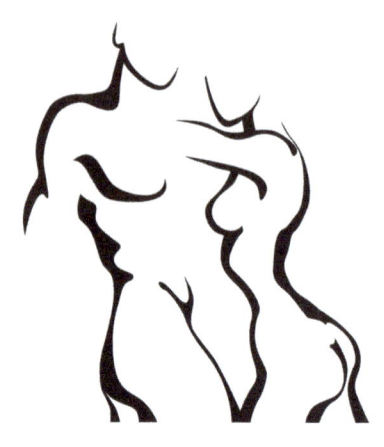

We poke, we pinch, and we pull. We see the worst in, and sabotage ourselves in many and various ways. Sometimes, we don't even realize we are doing it. Right?

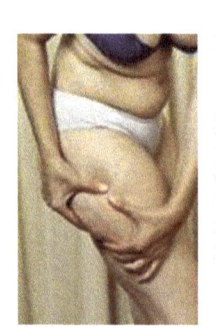

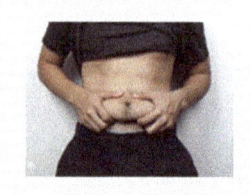

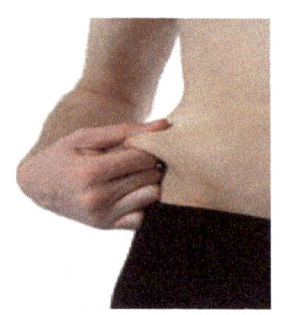

Negative self-talk is so toxic, and yet we still do it, even though we know how damaging it is to us! Over and over again, we mentally abuse ourselves by calling ourselves names, and putting ourselves down. Have you ever had these thoughts or feelings?

- I'm too old to do this!
- I can't believe I did that.
- I'm so stupid!
- I fail at everything I do!
- I'm not WORTHY
- I can't do this.
- You're not so cute anymore.
- I can't believe you thought she/he would call you back.
- My body is getting out of shape!
- I can't do anything right!

It's time to change that today. Start by putting yourself first and becoming your own best friend. The healing starts with *you*! Once you start treating yourself better, then better will appear—better friends, better opportunities and overall, a better lifestyle.

Remember, "You attract who you are." That's the magic of having better people around you. It starts with you!

The media doesn't help. All you hear is, "Look like her, look like him. Do this, do that, and you will be more attractive, sexier. Wear this perfume and you will be sexy. Wear this underwear and you will attract him or her." Really? Start paying attention: sex sells! In many shapes and forms. Sex sells, it's always been in marketing for some products, now more than ever!

We tend to forget that most of those celebrities and public figures who are on magazine covers, in movies, or anywhere in the public eye are covered in makeup and their photos are airbrushed to improve their looks and overall appeal to the fullest. I am happy to say that I have noticed more and more of these celebrities and public figures now acknowledging they are not as perfect as we see them. This is such a crucial admission; they are finally acknowledging they are normal like us. At the same time, it is sad that it took external influences for them to come out and admit this to the world. They too have many issues like anyone else. They deal with issues of self-worth more than ever! Yet most ads still encourage us to look like these fabricated images. What gloomy, mixed messages are being conveyed to people of all ages? I really try hard not to be influenced by commercials especially, as you will notice, they are always trying to talk you into something, whether good or bad. When we try to look like those celebrities and public figures in the media, we are pretty much guaranteed to fail.

Be yourself: everyone else is taken! – Oscar Wilde

Negative Body Image

Negative body image affects our self-esteem.
Let me ask you a few questions:
Are you after what the media promotes?
Do you have unrealistic goals?
Do you judge others?

Sometimes we can feel less beautiful than others may see us and sometimes we even have the nerve to judge others as less than beautiful. Who are we to judge? In fact, did you know they say we are born to judge? We just need to work on that part—the crucial part—not judging or we too will be judged! It's not easy, because as I mentioned, we are born to judge.

Did you know that someone with high self-esteem is more likely to succeed and be much happier than someone with low self-esteem? If you don't believe in yourself, who will?

I had heard on the radio that a woman who is prettier earns wages twenty-five percent higher than her peers, even though she's doing the exact same work as the woman sitting next to her? Know why? . . . It has nothing to do with her looks. We just assume it does because of what the media promotes. The one who has the higher self-esteem will demand higher wages because she or he will speak up and demand more. They believe they deserve more. While the person with lower self-esteem doesn't believe she or he deserves anything better. So, they don't get better. We are all beautiful in our own way. We are all unique just the way we were born.

What's beautiful to one, might not be to others . . .

"Beauty is in the eye of the beholder."

— Ancient Greek Origin

Warning signs to low self-esteem, which can lead to:
Eating Disorders (Bulimia/Anorexia)
Alcoholism
Drug addiction
Bullying of others
Self-hatred
Prostitution
Pornography
Dropping out of School/lower education
Teen pregnancy/early parenthood
Suicide attempts
Incarceration
Abusive relationships
Short-term employment/unable to keep a job

Do you agree these are signs of low self-esteem? Are there any others that come to mind?

All things in nature are beautiful in their own way.

When you see an elephant would you ever think it needs to go on a diet and lose weight? Of course not, as we are programmed to see them as big and bulky unless they're sick. We accept them just the way they are: big, strong, and beautiful.

We are all natural beauties just as we are—tall, short, bulky, skinny, or wide. Do you get the picture? Accept yourself just the way you are.

Here's one of the most empowering short stories I've read recently and wanted to share with you. The author is unknown, but its message is of utmost importance.

> *"As my friend was passing by these elephants at a fair, he suddenly stopped, confused by the fact that these huge creatures were being held by only a small rope tied to their front leg. No chains, no cages. It was obvious that the elephants could, at any time, break away from the ropes they were tied to, but for some reason, they did not. My friend saw a trainer nearby and asked why these beautiful, magnificent animals just stood there and made no attempt to get away.*
>
> *"Well," he said, "when they are very young and much smaller we use the same size of rope to tie them and, at that age, it's enough to hold them. As they grow up, they are conditioned to believe they cannot break away. They believe the rope can still hold them, so they never try to break free."*
>
> *My friend was amazed. These animals could at any time break free from their bonds but because they*

believed they couldn't, they were stuck right where they were.

Like these elephants, how many of us go through life hanging onto a belief that we cannot do something simply because we failed at it once before?

How many of us are being held back by old, out-dated beliefs that no longer serve us?

How many of us have avoided trying something new because of our limiting beliefs?

Worse yet, how many of us are being held back by someone else's limiting beliefs?

Don't be the elephant. You are the only one who is keeping yourself tied down. You can release yourself anytime you are ready to.

Let's move on to the work.

What do <u>you</u> see when you look in the mirror?

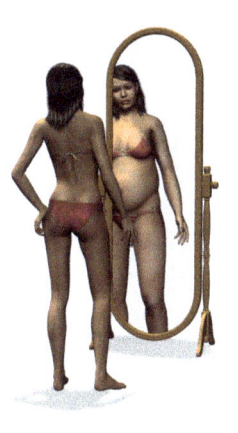

Look at this young woman. We see her in a certain way, as the beautiful woman she is. Unfortunately, she sees herself as the image in the mirror. There is a big difference between what we actually look like and how we see ourselves in the mirror.

Do you find more things that you like about yourself or that you don't like when you look in the mirror? Think about it: if I were to ask you to take one minute and think about things you don't like about yourself, would you have a problem coming up with any answers? Or if I asked you to take one minute and think about things you love about yourself, would you need more time? What you see and tell yourself is what you will eventually believe and become! As of today, can you please try to turn your negative thoughts about yourself into positive thoughts? It may be difficult at first, but with time you will begin to believe it and to see it! Just try it for twenty-one days. It may take time as you may have been having these negative thoughts your whole life. You can't expect to change overnight, but one day at a time. As they say, "Fake it 'til you make it!"

What triggers us to feel more or less beautiful?

Moving on: body image and beauty can be so *confusing* . . . don't you agree?

Opinions of Others

Physically, we don't change quickly, and yet . . . our looks can change in our mind and belief in seconds! For example, you can get out of bed in the morning feeling really bad. Then someone gives you a compliment and you notice your outlook and posture change just like that! Or, in reverse, you get up in the morning in a great mood feeling great about yourself. Then someone makes a negative comment about how you look or act which ruins your whole day. Right? Why? Because the feedback of others is so important to us?

Why does it matter so much what others think? It matters because we don't believe in ourselves. If we truly believed in ourselves and had high self-esteem, no one's feedback would really matter, would it? We wouldn't internalize it; rather, we would own who we are and be proud of who we've become!

Now let's talk about the power of friendship!

What do your friends say about you? Are your friends nurturing and trustworthy? Are you a good friend? For some of us, friends are very important. Our friends can encourage us in all kinds of ways, but what if our friend doesn't think our natural look or way is good enough? Could they actually encourage us into behaving negatively? Let me ask you this: what did your friend(s) say about you today? Was it positive or negative? How did that change your perspective? What message did you give your friend(s) today?

If your friends are so important in your life, and you really value their opinion, then you need to make sure you have true, caring friends that support and love you just the way you are!

If you really think about it, all we truly want is acceptance and acknowledgment. Sometimes we tend to say or do the wrong thing just to try to please others as we are craving acceptance. You need to be happy within yourself and stop trying to please others! Keep reminding yourself, you need to be your own best friend first!

Let's talk about diets, if there's still such a word! All we hear is, "Diet, diet, diet," "Beauty, beauty, beauty!" Do you think we are becoming self-conscious and upset with our weight and our beauty? If we could only live healthily in mind, body and soul, everything else would come so naturally with peace and love.

All too often, this is what we hear:

- Wear this. Don't wear that!
- Do this. Don't do that!
- Lose weight. Don't lose weight!
- You could use some plastic surgery.
- Look like this.
- Look like that actress.
- Try this makeup.
- Use this line-diminishing cream.
- You're so pale, go to a tanning salon.
- Get your hair done.
- Get your nails done.
- What's wrong with you?

What do you think about these comments? Do you receive these types of comments? Even after hearing them, we wonder why we sometimes feel like we're just not ever good enough.

Fashion, Cosmetic & Diet Industries

Let's move to fashion, cosmetic, and diet industries. Their goal is to make money: lots and lots of money! Their message seems to be that beauty is the key to love and success. They're rich because their goal is to make us feel unattractive, and make us believe that using their product(s) will make us attractive! Their message? Beauty is the key to love, success, and happiness.

In (2020) we got the biggest scare with COVID-19. Many had to go without. No one worried about buying new clothes, makeup, and glossy magazines then, did they?

Food was rationed: many of us only got what we needed if we lived near a store that had stock left. Do you think we worried about our looks or what size we were? Do you think anyone else spent hours on their looks or made sure their lip gloss was still on? Do we need a crisis like COVID-19 to wake us up to what is important? Many of us went back to our natural way and it felt so freeing!

Positive and Negative Influences:

Where do they all come from?

- ✓ An unhappy childhood?
- ✓ Traumatic experience?
- ✓ Experiences of failure?
- ✓ Negative self-talk?

Low self-esteem is a vicious cycle. Negative self-talk, self-blame, guilt, low performance, high anxiety—it's a circle of shame and guilt that we hang onto like that baggage we choose to carry from our past, our "old story." I could have stayed married and kept my old story: poor, unhappy me. I chose, however, to move on and believe in myself. This is what you need to do for yourself.

See this little girl? If I said to you in my loudest voice, "She's a stupid little girl! Look at her and those stupid curls and those fat cheeks." There she is crying again. How does that make you feel? Pretty angry, doesn't it?

So why is it okay for you to do it to yourself? Do you think it's abuse? Yes, of course it is. It's verbal abuse, and it's not okay for anyone to talk that way to you or to anyone else! Why is it okay for someone to say negative things to you? I can tell you over and over just how special and unique you are, but do you believe me? Remember, what you tell yourself you will eventually come to believe!

Take a minute and think of some of the negative things you say to yourself on a daily basis. The loudest voice you will ever hear is your own! Eventually, you start believing everything you say to yourself. So why not make them positive words and thoughts? It's that easy! Start a new, beautiful garden of thoughts. You deserve to be who you truly are.

Let me ask you this, when someone tells you that you are beautiful, do you reject the compliment or do you accept it and say "Thank you?" Some people may say horrible things to you, but it's what we choose to hear and believe that matters and how you choose to react to it. Will it affect your day? It is still your choice as to how you react? Yes! It's your *choice*!

When will you be ready for a positive change? You need to remember that others' opinions are not characteristic of who you are!

Tips to help you stay balanced:

Know that a number on the scale is not a measure of self-worth.
Don't compare yourself to others.
Identify who you are and be true to yourself.
Identifying your strengths and talents.
Acknowledge your value and worth.
Uncover your passions.
Stop compromising yourself by putting you and your needs on the back burner.
Look for the good in yourself and others.
Gratitude with attitude.
Remember the power of positive thinking.
Accept yourself just the way you are.
You control your thoughts. They don't control you!
You're the one who needs to care for yourself in a healthy way . . . You're in control!

High self-esteem = happiness within.

Once you accept who you are, just as you are, you automatically start loving yourself the way you are!

Once you accept yourself, you become motivated, ambitious, and fun to be with. You find yourself with future goals. You start having success in your relationships, career, and life goals! You start wanting to change your habits, eat healthier, and exercise more. It's contagious if you believe you can! Because you can!

Adjust the way you look at the world. It has made you the beautiful person you are today.

Compassion = happiness. If you are good to others, good will follow.

Every seed you plant will grow, so be aware of the beautiful seeds you plant in your mind more importantly, be aware of those weeds you allow others to plant there too!

Your thoughts shape who you are, shape your life.

"We become what we think about"

– Mark Twain

How you think will influence how you feel.
How you feel will affect your actions.
Your actions will lead to results, both negative and positive.
Remember, the loudest voice is your own.
You can be your worst critic.
Be positive and kind to yourself.
The most powerful tool you have is your own power of thought.

If we think about who we are and how we got here, we begin to believe in ourself and trust that every experience has made us the strong individual that we are today.

Let's test the power of thought. I want you to picture a bright lemon in front of you. Close your eyes and bite into it. Is your mouth watering yet? Your thoughts in general work in the same way. You can make them real, so very real that they can affect your life instantly in a negative or positive way, just as demonstrated with your thoughts of biting into that lemon. You get to choose which way to go. *It's your choice*!

Be Yourself

We all have our own individual unique bumps; it's time to embrace them all. We're all different, and that's what makes us beautiful individuals. It's time to be your own best friend!

Here are a few self-esteem formulas that work:

- ✓ Get rid of feelings of guilt.
- ✓ Let go of your frustration, your fears, and anger.

- ✓ Let go of your past; that's your old story. It's done!
- ✓ Replace negative messages with new, positive ones.
- ✓ You have the power. The power is yours to choose! Believe it.
- ✓ Realize the power of forgiveness—it's a gift to you!
- ✓ Stop buying into anyone's low, negative opinion of you.
- ✓ Create a vision of a life with no regrets.
- ✓ Everything you've been through has made you that much stronger and has made you the beautiful person you are today! Own it . . . be proud of it!
- ✓ Focus on what you have, not what you don't have.
- ✓ Gratitude with attitude is the secret.

Remember, it's your choice!

You Control Your Thoughts—They Don't Control You!

I remember when I first started studying hypnosis. I was so amazed and could not believe the power of the mind! I am still so astonished at what we can plant in our subconscious mind and most importantly, how easy it is!

I started looking at my own mind as a garden. Then realized I have the ability to really plant what I want to grow in my garden: after all, it's my own garden. Seeds or weeds, it's up to me to really choose which of them to keep or discard.

The power of planting my thoughts like a garden became easier and easier, but like a good gardener, I needed to care for it always. I needed to nourish it and pluck out the weeds by removing what is no longer needed. I found myself starting to manifest more easily with this concept and was amazed at my own power! I only let the positive into my garden space (seeds I will sow and nurture). When negative thoughts or the negative judgments of people attempt to creep into my garden, I visualize myself plucking them out, just like removing or pulling weeds in my flower garden. When I really take the time, I see colours, shapes and different sizes. I even see the old roots coming out. Like any good garden, you must cultivate it with love and care.

What does your garden look like?

Many of us want hypnosis, as you may believe it's the power of hypnosis that will help control your thoughts and eliminate undesirable habits or manifest whatever else you need to improve on. On the contrary, it's you that is in full control, all you. The difference is that you are now ready to be open to that change. You trust and are now ready to believe you can, as you are the one who is able to control it all. In a session of hypnosis, all we do is guide you to a positive you.

Staying on a Positive Track

You need to create new thinking patterns. I don't want to sound like I am judging, but this is especially relevant for the older generations like myself, the baby boomers, whose ancestors have instilled in us old, outdated patterns. For example, many of us were told, "Don't brag, because if you do, you are being conceited and you will jinx yourself."

I say, "Brag. You deserve to brag. You made it happen. Bragging provides positive reinforcement continuing to attract more of the same. Own it! Deserve it! Tell everyone how great you are, so more will flow. It's the law of attraction. Get rid of those old negative thinking patterns."

Let me share with you an old exercise I have used with my clients who are the negative thinkers in the room. It really works and I encourage you, if you are a negative thinker, to put an elastic band around your wrist. Snap the band on your wrist each time you think a negative thought or feel a negative emotion about anyone or anything including yourself. You may have heard of this one. It's an old tool, but a good one. Try it; you have nothing to lose except for your negative patterns and thoughts.

Most of my clients always reply by saying, "My wrist will be black and blue!" I respond by telling them not to worry: it won't. It will help you connect with how often you truly put yourself or others down. If you are experiencing any negativity, you snap! It's that easy, you'll see. After you snap, take a moment and change your negative thought to a positive. Remember, what you put out into the world comes back to you, so let's make it positive.

Try the elastic. You won't regret it. If anything, it's a good eye opener on how often you think or speak negatively. Hopefully you'll find that you are more positive, but this is a good tool to find that out.

Change

I am guessing you are ready for a change, otherwise you wouldn't continue to read this book. I truly believe that the tools come when you are ready. I am grateful to be a part of your healing journey. Thank you for having me.

Now let's continue to talk about positive energy which will continue to raise your self-esteem. We know that negative attracts negative. We also know that negative people thrive on bringing you under their dark cloud. Anyone coming to mind? Unfortunately, we all have someone like that in our life, we all do. It's up to you to decide how much time you really want to spend with that person, if any?

Beware of those so-called friends or family members with that negative energy who just want to suck you into their miserable dark spiral. Once you have decided you will no longer accept negative thoughts or actions from others, you will become more sensitive to the energy of others. Being in a positive vibe aura (or whatever you choose to call it) is the place we all want to be. When you maintain a positive frame of thought, you begin to see life in a different way. With all the work you have done so far from the other chapters, you will crave more positive energy and a happier lifestyle as well. It usually comes hand in hand with the work. Once you have completed all the work and heal yourself of your past with forgiveness, you will then see yourself in a different perspective, and will notice that everything else around you starts changing too. You'll see. When you become a better person, you attract better people. When you start loving yourself, more love will follow. When you allow peace to come into your life, more peace will follow.

Sometimes, you may even lose some friends or family members, as you may not see them as often. After all, you have changed in a more positive way and no longer agree with their perspective(s)/behavior(s) or have as much in common with them.

Sometimes this might not be a bad thing, don't you agree? At first it might be a bit difficult, as you may have to disrupt routines and perhaps some norms in your life. Remember that when you change, everything else will change in a more positive way.

We are all made of energy, so it's important to keep yourself surrounded by good energy. Once you are more balanced, more content within yourself, and you have learned and given permission to release your negative thoughts, you will notice your triggers will not show up as often, if at all. You don't need that negative drama in your life as you finally feel and believe you deserve better. Remember, you need to feel and believe you deserve it!

"When you truly feel and believe you deserve better, you do better. You attract better. You may have noticed that throughout the book I tend to repeat key information, as I, myself found this repetition was important for my own healing. I am doing this deliberately. Like anything else, keep doing it . . . repeat it until you get it."

You are one of a kind. That's pretty special, as no one is like you. No one on this planet is like you. Have you ever thought of that? Funny but true! How special does that make you feel? You should feel pretty special right now, because you *are* special.

Now it's time for you to start believing it, and owning it! You need to start planting these beautiful words that turn into positive feelings then positive actions, thereby growing your beautiful garden. As of today, you are choosing to plant, nurture, and grow that beautiful garden.

Grow it with much love and peace.

With much love
Lisa ox

What's Stopping Me From Being Happy?

Worthiness Mantra Circle

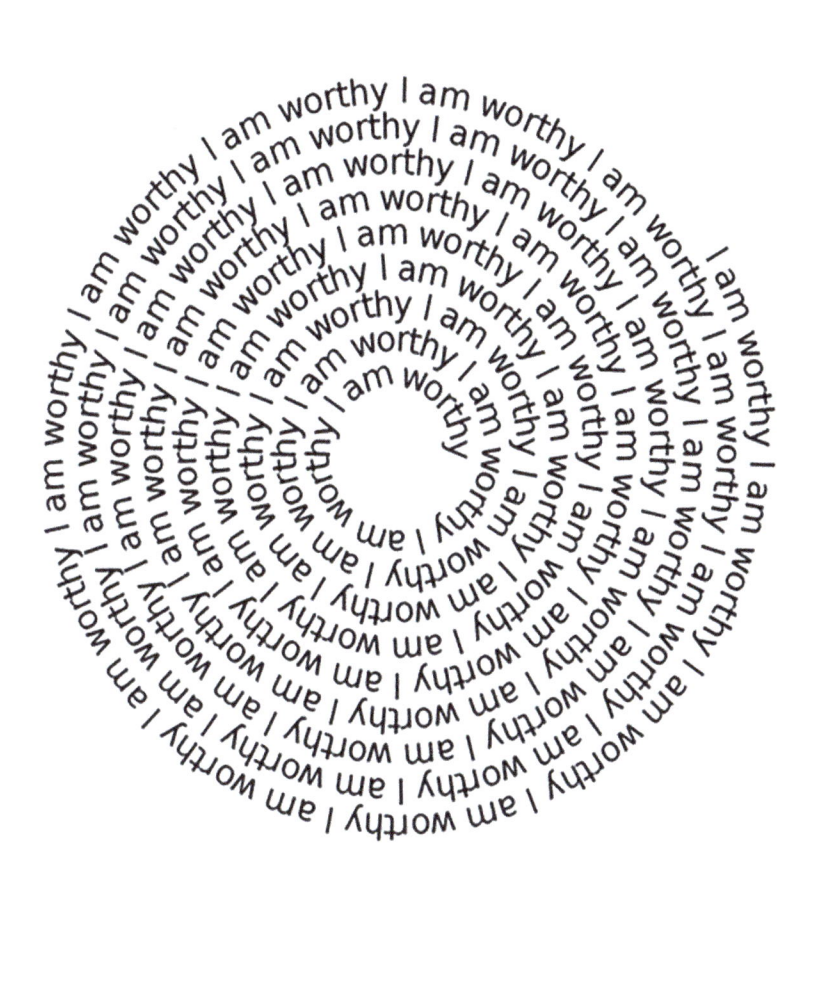

I am worthy I am worthy

Chapter 5

The Importance of Positive Energy

Negative Energy   Positive Energy

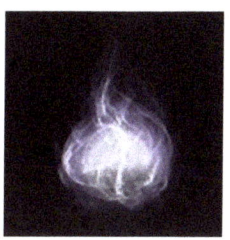

Let me ask you, why do you think good energy is so important? Every living thing is made of energy. We are all made of energy, so it's important to surround yourself with good energy. First you think it, then feel it, and then you act on it.

Negative and Positive Thoughts

When you are angry, you are unsatisfied.
When you are unsatisfied, no love comes your way.
When you dislike, something or someone you tend to judge.
When you judge, you become jealous.
When you are jealous, you become insecure.

When you are insecure, you tend to be insensitive.
When you are insensitive, you are selfish.
If you change one of these thoughts, what do you think will happen?

Positive thoughts = positive actions.

When you are happy, you tend to share love.
When you love, you want to share everything.
When you are contented, you are inspired.
When you are inspired, you always have beautiful energy.
When you have energy, you are fun, creative, and loved.
When you are loved, you are full of trust and faith.
Do you see how your feelings influence how you act, either negatively or positively?

Power of Negative Energy

Let's first talk about the power of negative energy.

Negative people tend to complain more often, have less energy, not sleep well, not plan ahead, be less healthy all around, and certainly tend not to be active or creative. They have a hard time maintaining any healthy relationships. They also have a hard time keeping a good job for a long period of time. The primary reason for this is because they really don't feel they deserve to have anything good in their lives. Deep down, they don't think they are worthy.

Negative people tend to keep company with others like them. They are under a dark cloud, just like the picture above, the black hole. They feel like victims, and for the most part, feel like the world owes them. They also feel like everything bad happens to them. They also talk and act negatively and make comments such as "I am so unlucky. Of course this would happen to me. Isn't that just my luck? If anything can go wrong it will with me. I am jinxed, I swear I am." Does this sound familiar? Do you know anyone like this in your life? Or, perhaps, is this you? If it's not you, then you know someone like this.

Spending time with negative people can be life sucking. What I mean by that is it can be very tiring, as they just want you to feel the same way they do. They drain the good energy right out of the room. Everyone around them gets sucked into it if you let them!

You will notice that negative thinkers are the first to take advantage of others. They always give themselves the upper hand, as it makes them feel better. The sad part is that they can change all this just by thinking differently. I know what you're thinking. "How?" As talked about in the earlier chapters, you need to really look at your actions and how you react to negative thoughts and feelings. Do you let it control you and your life?

Think back to something that happened to you that was negative. Have you recalled something? Did you bring it on with your fears? Most negative action is brought on by fear and anger. If you also notice, they tend to do much research supporting their position to prove that their negative view is documented fact. They also hold back any positive information that can offer an alternative solution to possibly change it to a more positive outcome.

Again, life is all about choices. Which way do you want to continue living your life? In a negative black hole that feels like you can't get out and life is just passing you by? Or finally say to yourself, "I can get out of this, and I will."

Changing Perspectives

Let's get started on your new healthier journey! As of today, I want you to do the following:

Each morning when you get up, you will say to yourself, "I love myself, and I'm so grateful for the beautiful person that I am. I'm ready. It's time. I'm ready to live a more positive, healthier lifestyle, the life I deserve. "

Each night before you go to sleep, you will say to yourself "I'm grateful for wanting better for myself, as I deserve to be happy and healthy. I'm grateful for all I have."

When and if you find yourself thinking or acting in a negative way, ask yourself the following:

What must I be thinking to achieve my goals?

_____

What must I be feeling to achieve my goals?

_____

The Power of Positive Energy

Now, we've talked a lot about negative energy, so let's address the power of positive energy. Once you get yourself thinking in a more positive way, you end up attracting more of the positive, just as mentioned in Chapter 1. The most important step is for you to believe this and once again trust that you are worthy of better in your life. You deserve it. Once you start believing this, everything comes to you in a much easier and more positive way because you are attracting it with your thoughts, but most importantly, with your feelings!

First you think it . . . then you feel it . . . then you act on it . . .

It's important for you to think, feel and act in a positive way. If you don't do this, you will find yourself sliding in and out of a slump, or as some may say, right back on that treadmill. You will find yourself unbalanced and overall not feeling good about your life as you are once again stuck in that negative hole. I can't say it enough; it's *your* choice! Remember what has been mentioned in the past chapters: life is all about choices. No one can take that away from you, one but you. *You* make the choice to get up in the morning and think positively, no matter what. I know it's hard some days, especially when you are not feeling good about yourself. "Fake it 'til you make it," or find at least one positive thing to focus on when you first get up. Many more positive things will start happening and just showing up.

You will notice once you are on a positive path, having made a positive choice that more than ever, you will become aware of negative energy around you, especially with others. Also, you will notice that negative people don't really want to be around you, as you are too challenging and meddling with their black hole. Overall, that's a great thing, as this is where you want to be in your life, in a more positive environment. Yes? Sometimes you might even lose a few family members or friends. Do you really want people like this to continue wasting your good energy? That's really what you are doing if you choose to be around them all the time; wasting your good energy and struggling to keep yours out of their black hole.

Once you are clear and feel you deserve to be happy and have more in life, it will follow. Once again, everything will fall into place. You will become more balanced, more content within yourself. You will have learned and permitted the release of your negative thoughts and negative triggers that once provoked anger and fear. You will notice they will not show up as often, if at all. Addressing your triggers is another healing process.

You won't need that negative drama in your life as you finally feel you deserve better. We all know life happens, and it's not always positive, but it's up to you how you react to the situation. It's up to you to choose how to react.

I wish you the best in your new way of thinking, your new healthier journey.

Life is still your choice. Choose wisely when you first get up.

Let me share with you some wisdom I received from an old Indigenous man who once asked me, "Lisa what side of the bed do you get up on?"

I said, "The right side."

He then responded, "Let me name your feet. Your right foot is called 'thank'. Your left foot is now called 'you.' Your first steps each morning are 'thank you.'"

What a wonderful way to start each morning!

With much love,
Lisa ox

Chapter 6
Self-Care

Self-care is not a luxury, it's a necessity.

Self-Care Suggestions

Stay off social media and all your electronics for a while, even just for a few hours per day.

Take time to just *be*, find yourself and connect within. Just love who you are today.

Enjoy your own company. At first it might be strange, feel empty, or you just may not be sure of what to do. You need to trust. The more you will do it, the more you will crave and need to do it. You will start enjoying yourself more and more with love.

As of today, no more negative thoughts or words about others. Try to find compassion. If not, just let it go. Negativity creates toxins within your mind, body, and soul.

As of today, do your best to no longer have negative self-talk! Negative thoughts and actions will take over your positive energy, if you let them. By continuing negative self-talk, you are feeding into negativity. You can look at negative talk as a fire burning beside you. The more you talk negatively, the more you are throwing wood on the fire. Then, of course, the fire gets bigger and bigger until it's out of control!

You control your thoughts: they don't control you.

As of today and each day going forward, give one compliment aloud to someone else. You will feel good about it, and it will help make that person's day. Good energy all around spreads like wildflowers! Try starting today.

Make time for yourself, minimally once a week. This might include saying no to others. Many of us tend to do so much for others and forget ourselves. When you have to say no, say it and don't hang on to the guilt. You deserve time for yourself, too. It might be hard at first, especially if you are the pleasing type, the type that always wants to help others be happy. That's not a bad thing, but stop putting yourself on the back burner. Happiness starts with you. After all, "If Mama Ain't happy, Ain't nobody's happy." Lindsey O'Connor .That's an old one, but a good one and so true.

Now, let's talk about apologizing. It's not always easy, but holding onto the anger, grudges, and frustration will only cause you to hold onto negative energy. The longer you hold onto it, the more damage it's doing to your own energy. Once again, you are just feeding your fire.

Stop being overly competitive. Dr. Phil once said, "Competing can quickly turn any relationship into an ugly battle. Can you possibly be a winner, if it is at the expense of making others losers? Solid relationships are built on sacrifice and caring not power and control. Competitiveness can drain the joy, confidence, and productivity out of any relationship."

Let's Talk a Little About Control

We tend to try to control everything; after all, no one can do it like I do? Right? We can be such control freaks and most of us won't admit it, but it's true. How often do we stay awake trying to figure out how to change this or that, her or him? How many times do we not listened to another person, because we are too busy giving out our great advice? We do this with our children, spouse, partner, friends, etc. So much is out of our control. Yet, we still think by wasting time worrying about it or sharing our opinions on what they should or shouldn't do, that we will somehow change it all . . .

Let's not forget how we know what's best for them, even if it's not always best.

Many of us have damaged good relationships, and yet we still try to control what has never been our business to control. It's really about power, control, and manipulation! Many of us have convinced ourselves that we don't want them to make the same mistakes we did. Sound familiar? The truth of the matter is no matter what we do, they will make their own mistakes, just as we did. That is what has made us the strong person we are today. The more you put that out there, the more it will happen.

"What you resist persists!"

– Carl Jung

Let's look at the synonyms for control:
Discipline
Domination
Force
Government
Jurisdiction
Management
Restraint
Restriction

These are just a few of the synonyms, trust me. Is that what we really want for our loved ones? Isn't control all about power?

We all know worrying is damaging to us, yet we all do it. I always tell everyone that worrying is like rocking in a rocking chair. You go back and forth, back and forth, yet change nothing. Time goes by, and you are still rocking. Yet we continue using that rocker, eventually damaging the chair over time. Isn't that what you are doing to yourself when you worry? You are not changing anything by going back and forth, just hurting yourself.

Let go. Leave it to your higher power. Allow others to make their own decisions: after all, it's their journey, not yours!

Gratitude with Attitude

Gratitude is such a powerful word.

As of today and each day going forward, the last thing you will do before you go to sleep is identify and say to yourself at least five things you are grateful for. The best part of this exercise is you will end your day and fall asleep with positive thoughts. First thing each the morning when you wake up, think of and say to yourself one thing about your life for which you are grateful and why you are so grateful to be alive and happy. Another good practice is to start a gratitude journal so you can always look back to remind yourself of all that is good in your life.

Before you go to sleep, let go of what is no longer serving you. Go to sleep, rest, and rejuvenate; after all there is nothing you can do about it now. Whatever it might be, release it to your higher power: to your angels, to Mother Earth, or to wherever you feel you have the faith and trust to let it go.

More Self-Care Tips

Here are more self-care tools for you:
Do things that bring you comfort.
Read a book.
Write in your journal.
Meditate. Bring peace.
Do your best at eating healthy.
Exercise as much as you can.
Join a yoga class—connect within.
Take a walk. Connect with Mother Earth.
Go to the park and just listen to the laughter.
Go to the airport and watch when people arrive—feel their joy.
Play your favourite music.
Take a long bath.
Find a beach and just be. Listen to the waves, and see the beauty around you.
Whatever you choose to do to nurture yourself is your choice.
This is *your* journey, so make it the best you can. You deserve self-care.

*With much love
Lisa ox*

Chapter 7

The Victim

How do we fall into the role of victim? Many of us live our whole life as a victim. Often it's the only way to be. We don't know any better, so we don't do any better. You can fall into this role at any age with any experience. It's like that beautiful story Wayne Dyer had told many times in many conferences that I also want to share, as I just love this story.

"A little story by Portia Nelson.

Portia was asked in a seminar to write her autobiography, but they said you only have one page to write it on. And you need to write it in five short chapters on one page. So, she wrote on one page and this is what she said:

Chapter 1

I walked down the street. There is a deep hole in the sidewalk. I fall in—I am lost, I am helpless, it isn't my fault. It takes forever to find a way out.

Chapter 2

I walk down the same street. There is a deep hole in the sidewalk, I pretend I don't see it. I fall down again—I can't believe I am at the same place, but it isn't my fault and it still takes a long time to get out.

Chapter 3

I walk down the same street. There is a deep hole in the sidewalk. I see it there, and I still fall in! It's a habit! My eyes are open. I know where I am. It is my fault. I get out immediately.

Chapter 4

I walk down the same street. There's a big hole in the sidewalk. I walk around it.

Chapter 5

I walk down another street."

This is the story of her life—the story of manifesting.

Those who play the *victim* never believe they are ever good enough. They don't like to make any decisions, as they don't trust their own judgement. If it was the wrong decision, they would have no one to blame but themselves. They feel weak and helpless. They often blame others for most of their mistakes and for not being where they had planned to be in their life. They feel everyone around them is negative, yet never take the time to truly look at themself, as they always tend to be the negative one. This is another example of the saying, "You attract who you are."

No matter what they have in their life, they tend to always complain and it's just never enough, no matter what is surrounding them. They normally have anxiety, as they're always in the past blaming someone or something, or in the future daydreaming of what and where they should be.

It is extremely difficult to be in the present, as that means they would have to look at themself, at what they have become now, taking ownership of who and where they are.

If they stay in the present, the blame game starts going around in their mind and all the negative emotions start. "It's his or her fault I am here," "I should have left a long time ago," etc. Victims can be verbally aggressive when they need to be, especially when it comes to bullying others; they can be great manipulators and control freaks. They tend to create unhappiness around them and drama tends to follows them as most of them thrive in it.

Their mission is to make others feel the same way they do, sometimes without even knowing it. They usually think they are right.

They love to play the "poor me" card, saying, "I am right." Many victims were brought up to be "good boys and girls," always obeying. Children should be seen but not heard; victims are used to feeling they are not important and are always looking and doing things to get attention. Unfortunately, victims tend to prefer negative attention, rather than none at all, just like any child when lacking attention. It is easy to take on the role of victim when one feels unimportant in the family home.

Most of the time, they continue whining like children suppressing their frustration and playing the blame game. Typically, you will hear comments such as, "Why do you treat me like this? I do everything for you! Why is my life this way? Why me?" They normally feel a lot of anger and jealousy. If they only realized their dysfunctional lives are a result of their own negative reactions and feelings! However, they keep suppressing and not dealing with their issues instead of healing. They tend to have difficulty with communication. As soon as they hear comments directed at them or are confronted by any finger pointing, they automatically shut down and stop the communication.

When they don't heal and take ownership of their past actions and reactions, that's when they tend not to move forward. They continue to attract the same people and relationships over and over again. After all: you attract who you feel you are!

Once they choose to take charge of their feelings and take time to heal by taking ownership of their life, they tend to change their role to that of a survivor.

The first step to healing from the victim role is forgiving themself. The second step is choosing to heal by forgiving others who have hurt them in any way. Victims are always stronger than they think. Once they take control of where they are and where they have been and own it, their healing journey begins. By taking ownership of their choices and actions they start believing they can change and be the person they've always wanted to be without guilt, blame, and shame.

Only once they deal with forgiveness and start working on their triggers from their past emotions can they choose to finally stop being the victim.

Once you start your healing journey you will discover "happiness is not by luck or by chance, it's not good fortune. It's a choice! It's your choice!" (Jim Rohn)

One thing we all have in common is choice! No one can take that away from you . . . no one but you. I always say to my students, "No one can ever take your choice away from you! We always have a choice. Always."

I know some of you are thinking, "I didn't choose to get beat up!" No, you are right. You didn't, but you did choose after that day, how you would react to it and how you would choose to let it affect your life and for how long. We always have the choice as to how we will react to what is happening in our life. We might not always like what is happening at the time, but truly we have the choice as to how we react and how we allow it to affect our lives.

We all have a story. Most of us have had something happen in our lives that we wish never did. If you take the time to look back and see yourself, I mean really look at yourself, you will see how that experience has made you who you are today.

Some choose to remain a victim for their entire life. Some choose to continue choosing life in the best way they possibly can. Ask yourself, "Which way do I choose to want to start my day today?"

I'd like you to take a moment to recall the experience I shared with you in Chapter five the Indigenous man naming my feet. How many of us take so much for granted . . . so much. I personally am so grateful to have legs to get up on, eyes to see God's beautiful canvas—so many things we take for granted every day. Once again, we have choice, right? Do we choose to get up with a positive or negative attitude each morning? Ask yourself in what mood do you normally get up? As of today, I would love for you to look into the mirror first thing in the morning and say, "Good morning beautiful/handsome."

I know you are thinking, "First thing in the morning I certainly don't always feel beautiful/handsome." When you start each day saying good morning beautiful/handsome, sooner or later you will find something else about you that is beautiful/handsome. Try it. What do you have to lose?

Are you ready to start your day with a good choice? Be grateful for each step you take on your journey. The past is the past: today is another gift to start over. As of today, start paying attention to and being aware of what is going on around you.

1. Ask yourself, "What do I need to do to start loving myself just the way I am today?"

_____

_____

_____

2. What is needed in my life for me to be contented just the way I am?

_____

_____

_____

Is it time to face it and own it? Let's start changing our attitude and the choices we make as of today.

Gratitude is seeing life as a gift. Life can be like a river. Sometimes it flows along so nicely, and other times it is impeded by a giant rock, a branch, or another obstacle. Eventually we figure out how to get around it, or it will eventually move out of our way, if we choose to remain there long enough. Just remember that life is short.

Change Expectation to Appreciation

Own who you were and who you are now! Be proud of yourself for getting here! You're doing the work, as you finally got tired of waiting for someone else to do the work for you! You are finally choosing to no longer be a victim, but choosing to be your own hero.

> Be good to yourself; fall in love with yourself all over again.
> You are the creator of your own life.
> Only you have control of your happiness.

With much love,
Lisa ox

Chapter 8
Triggers

What are Triggers?

Triggers can take many forms. We have five basic senses: touch, sight, hearing, smell, and taste any of these senses can trigger emotions (negative or positive).

Examples of Common Episodes that Can Bring Up or Set Off Triggers

<u>Negative Triggers</u>
- Any kind of stress
- Losses or trauma
- Frightening news
- Too much to do, feeling overwhelmed
- Family arguments
- End of a relationship
- Spending too much time alone
- Being judged
- Being criticized
- Experiencing teasing
- Being put down.
- Financial problems, getting a big bill

Positive Triggers

- Savouring pleasures
- Spending time doing things you enjoy
- Writing a gratitude list
- Cultivating optimism
- Kindness toward others
- Cultivating courage
- Finding meaning
- Pursuing passions and interests

Negative Emotional Responses to Triggers

- Guilt
- Fear
- Lack of Trust
- Frustration
- Anger
- Sadness
- Jealousy
- Resentment
- Ugliness

Positive Emotional Responses to Triggers

- Happiness
- Trusting
- Outgoing
- Love
- Safety
- Beauty
- Contentment
- Peacefulness
- Serenity
- Pride

› Inspiration

Memories play a large part in setting off triggers. Whatever memory you recall will trigger a positive or negative response. If negative responses keep coming up, it's because you haven't dealt with them and healed whatever situation those triggers originate from.

As of today, try your best to pay attention to your triggers and why they keep showing up. Each time a negative trigger comes up, take the time to write down information about the trigger. Use the following exercise to assist you.

1. What happened that set off my trigger?

_____

_____

_____

2. What are my most common feelings when a negative trigger is set off? (E.g., Jealousy, anger, frustration, etc.)

_____

_____

_____

3. When a trigger is set off, how do I react? (E.g., Do I yell and walk out?)

_____

_____

_____

4. How are these triggers affecting my life today? (E.g., I can't keep a relationship or a job, I lose my temper easily, etc.)

_____

_____

_____

Controlling Triggers and Healing

Now that you have recognized your triggers by putting them in writing, each time they come up, you might notice they are similar.

Basic Steps to Assist You in Controlling and Helping to Heal Your Triggers:

The first step is recognizing your triggers and taking ownership of them is by writing them down each time they pop into your life. This is part of healing and letting go. You need to feel it, then identify where the negative thoughts come from and why you are still allowing them to control your thoughts and actions. You need to *feel* to *heal*.

The second step, once you have written them down, is to read them over again and know that these are your feelings. Please don't belittle them or brush them off. They are obviously important to you, or you wouldn't be triggered.

The third step is to replace your negative thoughts and feelings with positive ones. Start feeling compassion for yourself; after all, you would do this for your best friend. Maybe it's time to treat you in the same way. Forgive those circumstances and people causing your emotional triggers, as you now are done with that old story. Take time to burn your written notes, to symbolically identify that you don't want to continue to carry that emotional baggage or experience those emotional triggers again. Those triggers are your old story. They no longer serve you.

The fourth step is to find a healthy outlet. You may want to go for a walk, read a book, meditate, whatever calms you down and helps you feel safe and content again. Remind yourself that those triggers are not a part of your new story and you choose not to waste any more energy on that old story.

The fifth step is to ask for guidance or call a friend. You don't have to do this alone. Treat yourself as you would your best friend. Get help.

Boundaries

Setting boundaries is important to others and most importantly to you. What does having boundaries mean? "Personal boundaries are guidelines, rules, or limits that a person creates to identify reasonable, safe, and permissible ways for other people to behave towards them, and how they will respond when someone passes those limits." –source (Wikipedia)

Let me start by asking, "Are you clear on your boundaries?" I mean, really clear? Many of us have never thought about them or given any thought to the importance of being clear on our boundaries.

How do you expect people to respect *your* boundaries, when most of us don't even know what our boundaries are? Most of us have never given it any thought, yet we expect others to know what lines not to cross. How can we expect those around us to treat us the way we want to be treated if we don't let them know what we expect and what lines not to cross? How can we expect others to know what our boundaries are if we're not even clear on them?

Communicate Your Boundaries

Clear boundaries equal self-respect. Knowing your limits and not letting others violate them reinforces your self-respect. Establishing your boundaries will release that big fat side of guilt, especially if you're one of those individuals who don't know how to say no. When you say yes to things you don't want to do, you will feel resentment toward *yourself* and the other *person*. There will always be someone who expects you to comply with their needs and wants. If you do and continue to do so, it's not fair to anyone.

I remember doing the following exercise years ago with Tashene Wolf. (Thank you, Tashene.) What an eye opener it was for me! When I did this exercise, I thought, "How can I expect anyone to not cross the line, if I don't know my own boundaries, my own limits?"

Boundaries Exercise

As you will notice on the exercise sheet, there is a small circle, which represents you. The big circle is where you will identify and document your boundaries. To begin, give some thought to what boundaries you have allowed others to cross that in retrospect you wish you never had? Given that, identify those boundaries that are now important to you, those that you will never let anyone cross again, e.g., being called names, yelled at, disrespected, used, etc.

Boundaries Exercise Worksheet

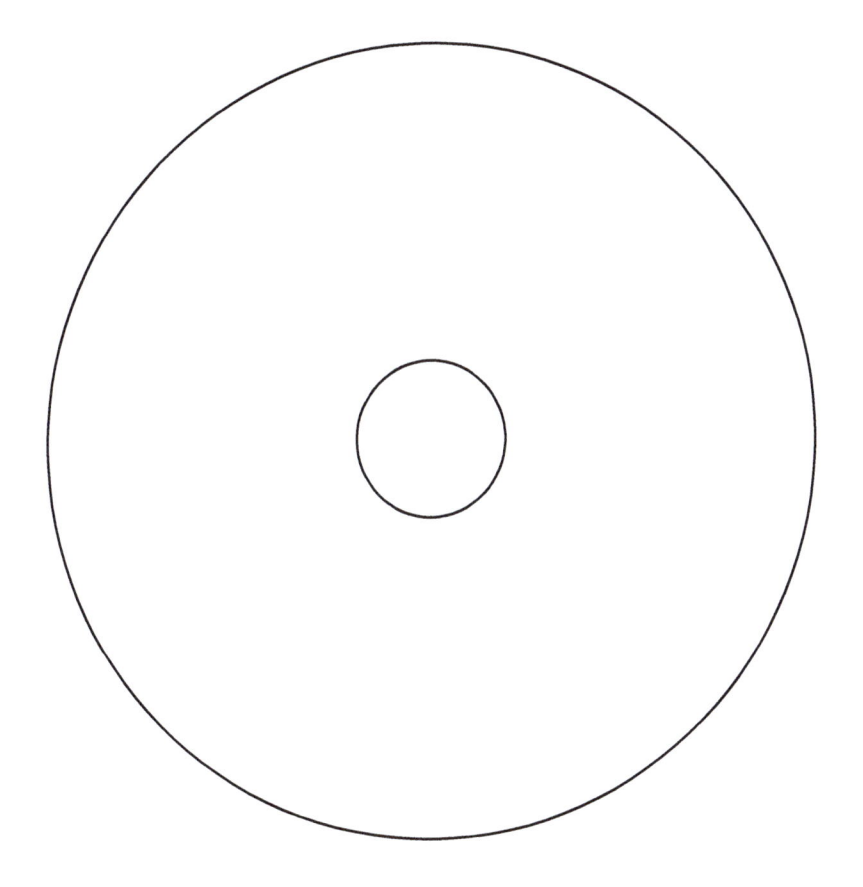

I hope you are as fulfilled and as clear as I was when I did mine. Now you know what is not to be crossed in any of your relationships at home, at work, on friends' outings, etc.

Let's move on to the *Circles of Life exercise*. This exercise is for you to look at the people you have attracted into your life and why. It will help you gain clarity on who is around you and whether they are good for you or toxic. Again, I did this exercise several years ago with Tashene Wolfe and realized there were people in my life that weren't really kind, respectable or beneficial to me at that time. In identifying this, I felt I didn't need to continue maintaining some friendships or relationships as I was wasting my good energy and not getting anything back. I know it sounds cold and selfish, but it takes two to foster a good relationship.

1. Using the Circles of Life diagram on the next page, write your name in the middle circle. Then write down everyone that is in your life from those closest to you (in the bigger circles) to those not so close (in the smaller circles).

2. Now look at each circle and ask yourself the following questions: "Is this a healthy relationship?" (Each time I am around this person do I feel sadness or happiness? Do they make me feel inadequate or powerful each time I see them or talk to them?)

Circles of Life Exercise Worksheet

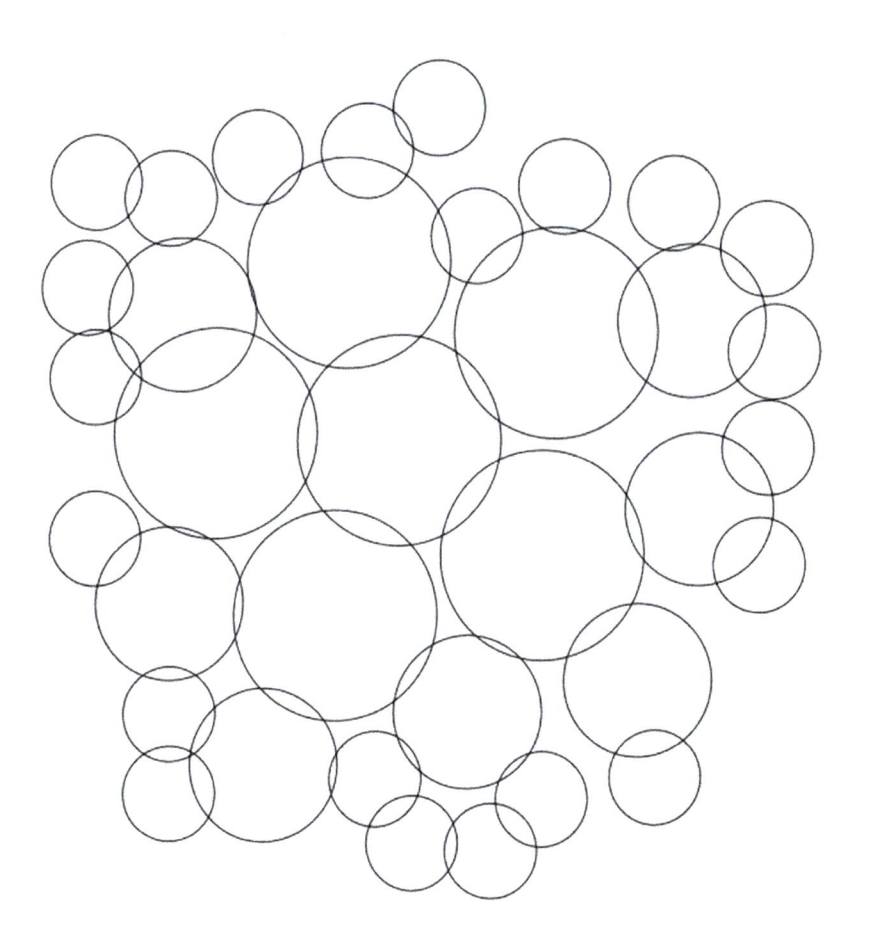

3. Now ask yourself what the other person is putting into your relationship. (Am I always the one who goes out of my way to keep this relationship going? Am I here out of guilt? Am I always calling them, or are they doing a good job in communicating to keep this relationship going?)

_____

_____

_____

4. Is this a good fit or is your friend toxic? How much of yourself do you need to give up having this individual in your circle? (Each time I am with them, do I feel I need to drink excessively? Does she or he make me feel like I am a party pooper? I cannot be with this person too long, as I always doing something I regret later. Or do we always do healthy, positive, and relaxing things when we are together?)

_____

_____

_____

5. What is that person taking from you or what are you taking from them? (Do I feel like I am always paying or driving everywhere and they never offer, or do I feel this relationship is equal we tend to do for each other?)

_____

_____

_____

These are only some examples to help you know your family and friends better. You know what to ask yourself. All of these circles represent the people around you, the environment you live in. Do you trust them? Is everyone currently in your circle supporting your best interest, or do you keep him or her in your life because of your old story, or out of guilt?

I hope you found this exercise an eye-opener. I know I did. It helped me clear out the weeds, I guess I would say. It made me realize that I had people in my life that I thought were good, but truly were not.

Imagine that your life is like driving a car. If you are always looking in your rear-view mirror, what do you think will happen? Eventually you will hit something in front of you and get hurt. If you continue to look behind, you can't move forward.

I would like to close this chapter with this beautiful Serenity prayer, which I use often to help to let go of what no longer serves me whenever needed. -

*"God grant me the **Serenity**
to accept the things I cannot **Change**;
Courage to change the things I can;
and **Wisdom** to know the difference."*

-Reinhold Niebuhr-

I AM Meditation

As we near the end of this healing book, there is no better way to close off our healing journey together but with my favourite meditation, "I AM."

My last question to you today is; "what kind of (I AM) is coming out of your thoughts, feelings and your voice?"

I recommend you record yourself and listen to this powerful "I AM meditation," whenever needed. By you listening to your own voice, you will feel more connected and committed to become the positive "I AM" that you choose. You become exactly what you believe with the power of "I AM." Words create power.

Words are like electricity, if you use electricity the right way, it gives us light and power. When used the wrong way, it can be very dangerous, and it can harm you just like negative "I AM."

When you say to yourself "I am Beautiful," beauty comes looking for you. When you say, "I am loved," love comes looking for you. When you say, "I am peaceful," peace will come looking for you, and so on.

The power of "I AM," what follows these two simple words, "I AM," will determine what kind of life you will live, negative or positive. As of today, please be aware of what follows your "I AM."

With much love "I AM meditation"

Get yourself comfortable and just relax. Relax and enjoy this healing session you're about to receive. Be open to receive.... and just let go, trust and have faith that you will receive exactly what you need today and this day forward. Give your thoughts and body permission to just let go, let go and just relax. Take a nice deep breath in and release. Listen to the powerful words of "I AM." With love.

I am present, I am present, I am
I am worthy, I am worthy, I am
I am peace, I am peace, I am
I am love, I am love, I am
I am grateful, I am grateful, I am
I am forgiven, I am forgiven, I am
I am light, I am light, I am
I am kind, I am kind, I am
I am healthy, I am healthy, I am
I am strong, I am strong, I am
I am young, I am young, I am
I am vibrant, I am vibrant, I am
I am unique just the way I am, I am unique
I am happy, I am happy, I am
I am bountiful, I am bountiful, I am
I am blessed, I am blessed, I am
I am beautiful, I am beautiful, I am
I am whole, I am whole, I am
I am capable, I am capable, I am

All through the day and night the power of "I AM" is at work. I trust, I believe and I let go.

I am that I am
I am a masterpiece, I am a masterpiece, I am
I am wonderful, I am wonderful, I am

I am one of a kind, I am one of a kind, I am
I am lovable, I am lovable, I am
I am intelligent, I am intelligent, I am
I am creative, I am creative, I am
I am powerful, I am powerful, I am
I am healthy, I am healthy, I am
I am excited about my future, I am excited, I am
I am grateful, I am grateful, I am
I am at peace, I am at peace, I am
I am love, I am love, I am
I am grateful for all that I am
I am that I am

As we slowly end this healing meditation of relaxation, slowly come back, come back to your breath. Returning to your body, take a deep breath in and just let it go. Feel your body, your energy, and your peace come within stronger than ever. Allow your body to heal what needs to be healed, trust and have faith to just let go.

Whenever needed you can come back to this state of peace and love, whenever needed. Breathe in peace, breathe in love, breathe in gratitude and exhale what no longer serves you.

Have faith and let go… let God. Let go to your Higher Power. Trust once again that you have just received whatever is needed today and this day forward.

These peaceful loving words are to bless your future.

Trust, have faith and know that everything you need is within you.

With many blessings

Lisa Marie Ellis

I am that I Am.

– Exodus 3:14

*With much love
Lisa ox*

About the Author

Lisa Ellis (Also known as "Passion Lady")

Lisa's motivation and interest in spiritual healing started in her youth. She has fond memories of her father and recalls, "My father, Sylvio LeBrasseur, was a healer.. For some reason, throughout my life, I have been curious and drawn to spiritual healing in many different aspects. It seems to be all around me and comes to me freely."
Lisa began this journey over twenty years ago, focusing on connecting with others on a much deeper spiritual level. For over two decades, Lisa has offered a series of presentations and workshops designed to enhance various personal life skills and passions; skills that contribute significantly to individual growth, self-awareness and self-esteem. Lisa is very passionate and committed to helping people make positive changes in their lives. It gives her great pleasure to see those she has helped, become enlightened and blossom before her eyes. The greatest reward is when she learns of how grateful people are and how their lives have changed in such a positive way.

Lisa was very fortunate to be certified as a yoga teacher in the birthplace of Hatha Yoga, Rishikesh, India at the Nada Yoga School (1995). Lisa has been trained by some of the greatest teachers, including Dr. Sharron Forrest, in both Peru and Canada. She was also trained by Dr. Jivasu in India, as well as, Canada. Lisa had the pleasure of being personally facilitated by Janet and Chris Attwood to teach the Passion Test. She is also trained as a Life Coach and is a certified hypnotherapist and holds various other certifications.

The Ho'oponopono prayer—This prayer I share with you as it has helped me through so many difficult times. If ever you are angry, frustrated and want forgiveness from another, you need to first, forgive them. USE THIS. It truly works. You will feel peace encompass you as you repeat these words (mantra): An Ancient Hawaiian Prayer

"I'm *Sorry*.

Please *Forgive* me.

Thank you, I *Love* you."

"All things are possible for one who believes."
Mark 9:23,

Thank you for gifting me this opportunity to be a part of your new journey.

With much Love
Lisa ox

CPSIA information can be obtained
at www.ICGtesting.com
Printed in the USA
BVHW090930271021
619747BV00004B/109

9 781039 105317